For Duane,

Thirteen years, and every day
is still like the first.

Special Thanks to...

Liz Dobecka and Timeless Blooms,
for letting me use the business one
more time. I faked the phone and
e-mail this time, so maybe you
won't get requests for support.

Courtney and Michael, the happy
couple. The beauty of your special
day makes my work look that
much better.

Rebecca Gulick, Kate Reber, and
Liz Welch, for making it look like
I understand punctuation.

And, finally, Marjorie Baer. Let's
stop kidding ourselves; I can never
make it up to you.

contents

contents

contents

introduction

The Visual QuickProject Guide that you hold in your hands offers a unique way to learn about new technologies. Instead of drowning you in theoretical possibilities and lengthy explanations, this Visual QuickProject Guide uses big, color illustrations coupled with clear, concise step-by-step instructions to show you how to complete one specific project in a matter of hours.

Our project in this book is to create a beautiful, engaging Web site using Adobe Flash CS3 Professional. Our Web site showcases a small, home-based business, but since the project covers all the basic techniques, you'll be able to use what you learn to create your own Flash-based Web sites—perhaps to promote your own business, showcase a hobby or collection, or provide a site for your neighborhood association.

what you'll create

This is the home page of the Timeless Blooms Web site, the project you'll create. In the process, you'll learn the following useful techniques:

Draw graphic elements to define your site's look and feel.

Use special text containers to process user input and load text dynamically.

Create interactive buttons for navigation between the different sections of your site.

Animate text to provide interest and a professional quality.

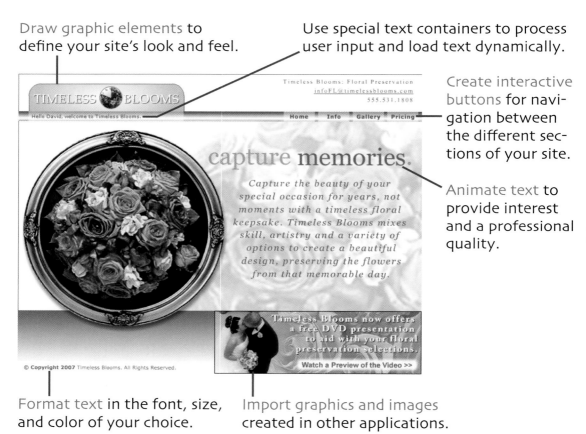

Format text in the font, size, and color of your choice.

Import graphics and images created in other applications.

mport video, including cue points that trigger changes in your movie.

Parse XML files to create a dynamic photo gallery.

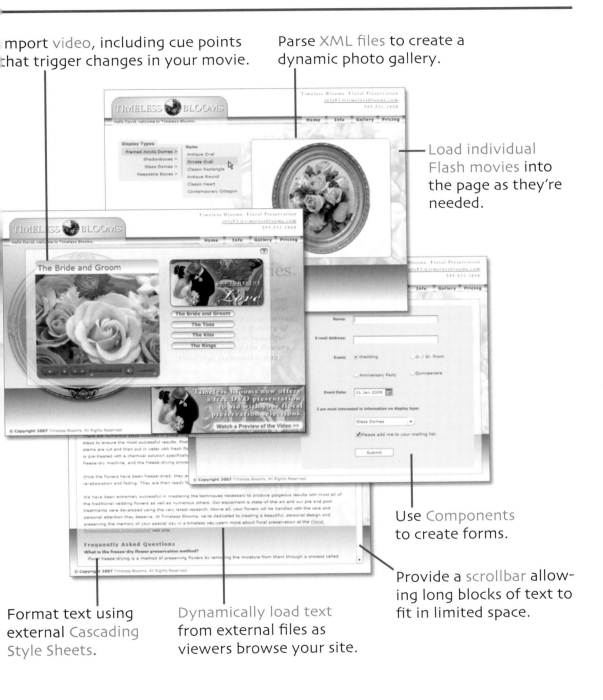

Load individual Flash movies into the page as they're needed.

Use Components to create forms.

Provide a scrollbar allowing long blocks of text to fit in limited space.

Format text using external Cascading Style Sheets.

Dynamically load text from external files as viewers browse your site.

how this book works

The title of each section explains what is covered in that section.

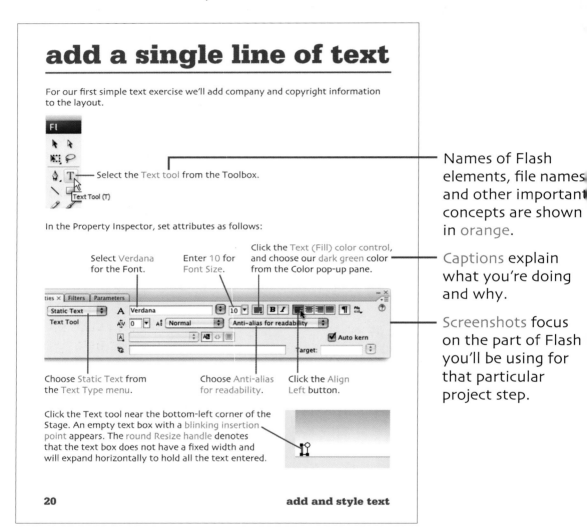

add a single line of text

For our first simple text exercise we'll add company and copyright information to the layout.

Select the Text tool from the Toolbox.

In the Property Inspector, set attributes as follows:

Select Verdana for the Font.

Enter 10 for Font Size.

Click the Text (Fill) color control, and choose our dark green color from the Color pop-up pane.

Choose Static Text from the Text Type menu.

Choose Anti-alias for readability.

Click the Align Left button.

Click the Text tool near the bottom-left corner of the Stage. An empty text box with a blinking insertion point appears. The round Resize handle denotes that the text box does not have a fixed width and will expand horizontally to hold all the text entered.

20   add and style text

Names of Flash elements, file names and other important concepts are shown in orange.

Captions explain what you're doing and why.

Screenshots focus on the part of Flash you'll be using for that particular project step.

The extra bits section at the end of chapters contains additional tips and tricks that you might like to know but that aren't absolutely necessary for creating the Web page.

extra bits

reusable graphics p. 26

- Using symbols in Flash provides two main benefits: reduced file size and ease of editing.

  When you create a symbol and place instances of that symbol on the Stage, your movie's file size is reduced because no matter how many times you use it, the code required to define it is only included in the file once. Each instance just points to the symbol and describes any modifications to that symbol, such as transparency or size.

  Modifying work later is also much easier. Imagine that you've placed 100 blue squares (not instances of a blue square symbol) throughout your movie, and then you decide to change the color. You have to find and change all 100 squares. But if you made a symbol of a blue square and placed 100 instances, you only have to change the symbol, and the 100 instances are updated automatically.

symbol-editing mode p. 30

- When you have an object on the Stage that is a container for other objects (groups, symbols and text boxes), you can just double-click it to "get inside" and edit the contents.

- To exit the editing mode of the container, you can double-click outside the bounds of the container.

transform objects p. 31

- When you're scaling vector objects (those drawn in Flash or imported from Illustrator or Fireworks, as in the logo file) you can increase or decrease the size without negative effect. However, if you're working with a bitmap image, you'll want to avoid enlarging it. An enlarged bitmap has to be resampled and can become distorted or fuzzy. It's best to open the image in an image editor such as Adobe Photoshop and scale it to the size you need.

The heading for each group of tips matches the section title. (The colors are just for decoration and have no hidden meaning.)

Next to the heading there's a page number that also shows which section the tips belong to.

work with imported objects

companion web site

You can find the companion Web site for Creating a Web Site with Flash CS3 Professional: Visual QuickProject Guide at: http://www.davidjmorris.com/vqj/flash

In the Asset Files section of the site, you'll find all of the files you need to complete the project in this book. You can also download the intermediate files created in each chapter and the files that make up the final project site.

Visit the Completed Project Site section to see a completed example of the site you're building in this book.

You can also find any updated material in the Corrections section of the site.

explore flash

At first glance the Flash interface can be overwhelming with its many panels and controls, but don't be concerned. As you progress through this project, you'll learn how to access the important stuff and how to harness all the power of Flash. When you finish the project, you'll have the knowledge and skills needed to create a professional-quality Web site to suit your business, organization, or personal needs.

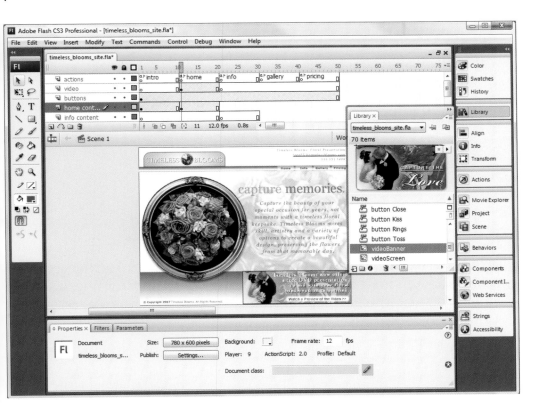

Flash borrows many of its conventions and terms from film production. The presentation you create for viewers is a movie, the distinct parts of the movie are scenes, the players (your content) are on the Stage, and movement through time is accomplished via the Timeline. Thinking about the Flash interface in the context of this film metaphor will help you quickly grasp the way we work in Flash. We are producing a movie that features your content and tells the story you want Web viewers to see. (See extra bits on Page xx.)

explore flash (cont.)

The story you're telling with your movie is presented on the Stage. You'll use it as your workspace to place and arrange the elements of your site. The Stage's rectangular dimensions define the area of your movie that viewers will see.

Edit Bar

Gray space around the Stage makes up the Pasteboard, which holds objects that hang off the Stage and animated elements that move onto or off of the Stage. To view or hide objects on the Pasteboard, choose View > Work Area, or press Ctrl Shift w (Windows) or ⌘ Shift w (Mac).

In Flash, you'll often find yourself drilled down multiple levels within elements, such as editing text that is inside a button symbol inside a movie placed in a particular scene. The Edit Bar above the Stage displays those levels to help keep you oriented and to let you quickly backtrack when your edit is complete. Additionally, you can use it to show and hide the Timeline, to navigate between scenes, to locate and modify symbols, and to change view magnification.

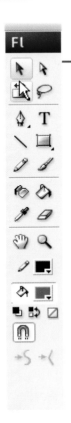

The Tools panel is the toolbox you'll use to draw objects, create text, and modify the elements of your movie. The Tools panel also lets you change your view of the Stage, modify colors, and set options for the tools you choose.

Review and change the attributes of objects in the Property Inspector. Controls in the Property Inspector change dynamically, displaying the attributes and settings relevant to your current selection. Here you'll be able to modify the attributes of text, graphics, frames, animations, and more.

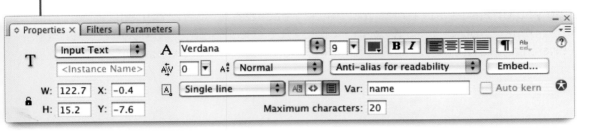

explore flash (cont.)

The Timeline controls the order, timing, and flow of your movie. The panel contains three primary sections: frames, layers, and the Playhead.

The Playhead indicates the current frame displayed on the Stage.

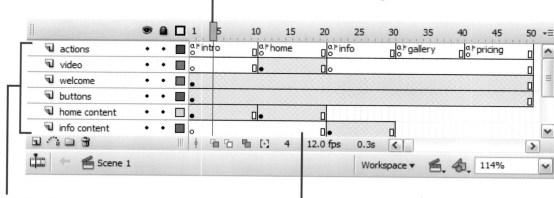

Think of layers as independent strips of film, each containing its own objects, stacked on top of one another, and composited to present a particular frame. In most cases, each layer we create will contain only a few objects, making it easier to keep track of things as the project gets progressively more complex.

Frames in the Timeline represent changes in your content over time. However, it's important to think of frames as something more than just for animation; frames also serve an important function as milestones within your site to which you can link other content.

If the elements in your movie are the players, then symbols are the featured stars. Using symbols decreases file size, saves time on edits, and organizes your file. The symbols in your movie are stored and accessed from the Library panel.

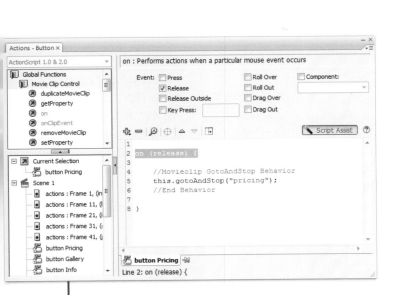

The Actions panel is used for adding ActionScript to your movie. ActionScript is Flash's scripting language for adding complex interactivity, controlling naviga-tion, and programming many of the advanced functions found in robust Flash applications. As you can imagine, it can be a daunting task to script a movie, but don't worry. We'll use the simplified process provided in the Behaviors panel and use the Script Assist feature in the Actions panel.

explore flash (cont.)

The Behaviors panel provides the power and control of ActionScript without your having to code the script yourself. Behaviors are prepackaged bits of ActionScript presented with interfaces that allow you to easily set up complex interactions that would otherwise require coding.

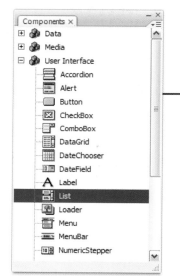

If Behaviors are packages of ActionScript that you apply to objects in your file, components, accessed from the Components panel, are packages of special-purpose objects that include the ActionScript to control their behavior. Components include simple user interface controls, such as buttons and checkboxes, and more complex controls that contain content, such as scroll panes, windows, and video players.

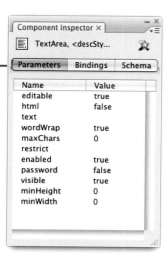

After you add a component to your file, you'll use the Component Inspector panel and the Parameters tab of the Property Inspector to specify parameters specific to the component type and your particular design requirements.

the next step

While this Visual QuickProject Guide teaches you the basics for creating a Web site in Flash, there is much more to learn. If you're curious about Flash development, try Flash CS3 Professional for Windows and Macintosh: Visual QuickStart Guide (ISBN 0-321-50291-4), by Katherine Ulrich. It features clear examples, simple step-by-step instructions, and loads of visual aids to cover every aspect of Flash design.

After that, you can take it to the next level with Flash CS3 Professional Advanced for Windows and Macintosh: Visual QuickPro Guide (ISBN 0-321-50303-1), by Russell Chun.

extra bits

explore flash p.xiii

- Avoid the temptation to "store" unused objects offstage on the Pasteboard; they'll still be exported in the final movie and will add to the file size, prolonging download times.

- Dragging the gripper in the bottom-right corner of the Property Inspector allows for hiding the bottom half of the panel, which contains controls that are considered secondary. Hiding these controls is not recommended for the novice so that you don't waste time hunting around the application when you do need them.

- Need a custom user interface element that's not included in Flash installed components? Many custom components can be found on the Adobe Exchange for you to download and install. The Exchange is located at: http://www.adobe.com/exchange.

introduction

1. prepare your site files

Before you begin the design and development of your Web site, it's important to get organized.

In this chapter, we set up a directory structure for all of our files, create and save the Flash file that will be our site movie, and define and save the color scheme that we'll use throughout the site.

If you haven't already done so, download the asset files for the Timeless Blooms Web site from this book's companion site at www.davidjmorris.com/vqj/flash.

define folder structure

Before beginning work on our Flash movie, you need to set up a hierarchy of folders and files on your computer's desktop. Within this structure we'll have two discrete folder sets: one for files that we'll use during the development of the site and one for files that will be uploaded to the Web.

From the Windows Explorer or Mac OS's Finder, choose File > New > Folder to create the parent directory. Name the folder timeless_blooms_website

Open the timeless_blooms_website folder, and create two new folders. Name one site_files and one development_files.

Copy the asset files that you downloaded from this book's companion site into the development_files folder.

create your site file

There are two types of Flash files that we'll be working with. A FLA file is the working file you create in Flash and do all of your design and development in. FLA files are opened only with Flash. At the other end of the process, a SWF file is the file you export from Flash and post on the Web. The SWF file is your Flash movie and can be opened by browsers, the Flash Player, and some other applications.

Launch Flash, and choose File > New to create your FLA file.

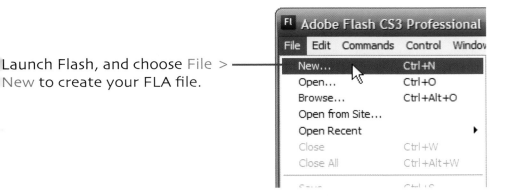

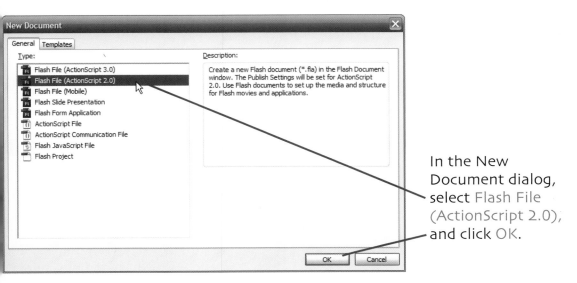

In the New Document dialog, select Flash File (ActionScript 2.0), and click OK.

set document properties

Flash defaults to a canvas size of 550 x 400 pixels with a white background. We can change those settings to fit the needs of our project and add information describing our site for Internet search engines while we're at it.

If the Property Inspector is not visible, choose Window > Properties > Properties to open it.

In the Property Inspector, click the Document Properties button. This is a bit confusing, since the button is next to a label that reads Size and the text on the button shows the canvas dimensions. Even so, this is the Document Properties button.

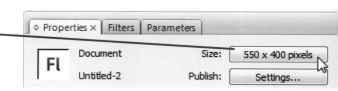

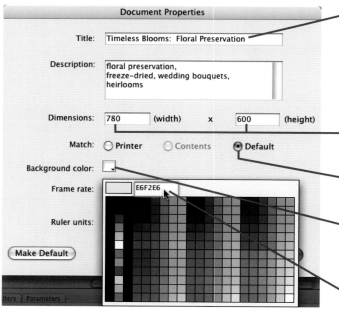

1 In the Document Properties dialog, enter Timeless Blooms: Floral Preservation for the Title and floral preservation, freeze-dried, wedding bouquets, heirlooms in the Description field.

2 Enter 780 for the width and 600 for the height.

3 Confirm that Default is selected as the Match value.

4 Click the Background Color control to open the pop-up swatches pane.

In the Hex Edit text field, select the text #FFFFFF, replace it with E6F2E6, and press ←Enter.

5 Click OK to exit the Document Properties dialog.

prepare your site files

save your file

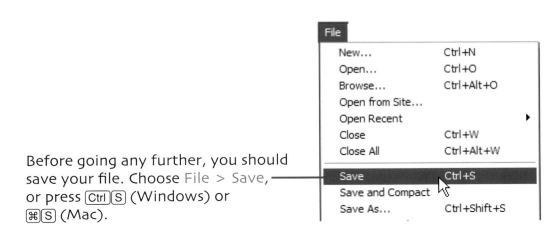

Before going any further, you should save your file. Choose File > Save, or press [Ctrl][S] (Windows) or [⌘][S] (Mac).

In the Save As dialog, navigate to the development_files folder we created earlier. Enter timeless_blooms_site.fla for the file name, and click Save.

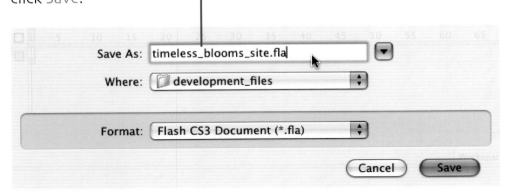

I'll remind you to save your work at the end of each chapter, but you should keep in mind the old edict "Save early and often."

load a workspace

If you are like me, when you install a new application on your computer you like to go exploring, trying different functions to see what they do. In doing so, panels and controls get moved all over the workspace, making for a very cluttered and ineffective work area.

You can return the panels to the default layout by choosing Window > Workspace > Default.

You may also gain valuable work area by collapsing panels to icons. I suggest collapsing to icons with descriptive text until you become familiar with the application, and then collapsing them further as you proceed.

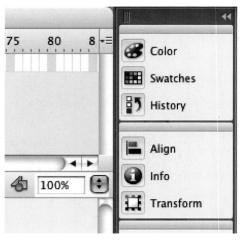

To collapse the panels to icons with text, choose Window > Workspace > Icons and Text.

Additionally, as you become more accustomed to Flash development you will realize that development occurs in stages where some panels are needed and others are not. You can customize and save workspaces to switch for different phases.

prepare your site files

save your color scheme

To make applying our color scheme easier and to speed development, we'll first add the colors for our site to the Color Swatches panel, where they can be easily accessed from any of Flash's pop-up swatches panes. (See extra bits on Page 8.)

1 In the Panels Dock click the collapsed Color panel icon to open the Color panel. Click the paintbucket icon to highlight the Fill color selector.

2 To define the dark green color, enter the hex color value 448855 in the Hex value field. Press ←Enter.

3 On the right of the panel's title bar, click the Options menu icon, and choose Add Swatch.

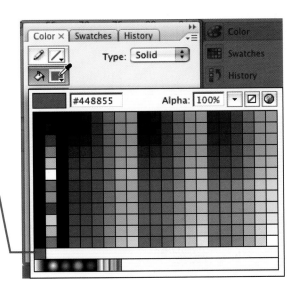

Click one of the color wells in the panel to open the swatches pop-up. Notice that our dark green color has been added to the bottom row of swatches.

Repeat steps 1 through 3 to add the other colors to the swatches.

Medium Green: 669966

Dark Purple: 883399

Medium Purple: 994499

Light Purple: BB99CC

Orange: FF8833

Click away from the panel to collapse it back to the dock.

prepare your site files

extra bits

save your color scheme p. 7

- Choosing the color scheme for your Web site is an important first step in the design phase of development. Here are a few tips to keep in mind:

  Limit the number of colors used in your design. Too many colors make the design look chaotic and cluttered.

  Pick two or three main colors, and then use different tints of those colors for highlights, backgrounds, etc.

  If your organization has a color logo or a primary graphic for the home page, pull colors from that existing artwork, or choose colors that are complementary.

prepare your site files

2. design the layout of your stage

Our first task in Web site development is to design the visual framework within which all of our content will be presented. Think of it as dressing the set of your movie: providing the backdrop, defining different regions, and making it visually attractive. Along the way we'll learn how to use many of Flash's most basic functions. The following are some of the tasks we'll cover:

Create and modify radial gradient fills.

Draw and modify Graphic Primitives.

Use drawing tools to create layout elements.

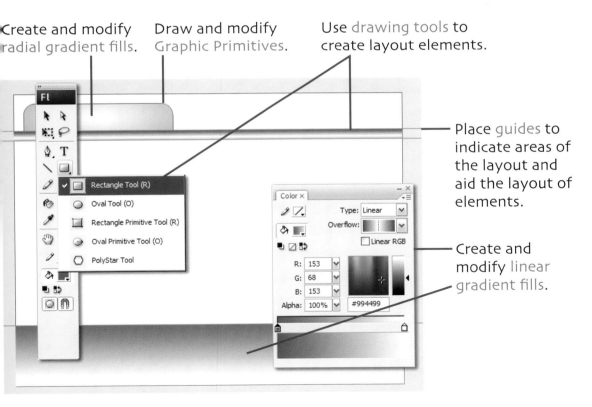

Place guides to indicate areas of the layout and aid the layout of elements.

Create and modify linear gradient fills.

set up guides

Using guides in your file helps you define areas of your Stage and eases placement of objects. Let's add some guides before we begin drawing our background. To ensure correct placement of the guides, we use the Info panel in the expanded state so that it is available for multiple actions.

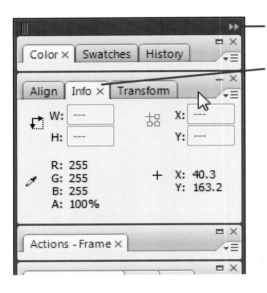

1 Click the double arrow at the top of the Panels Dock to expand panels.

2 If the Align/Info/Transform panel group is expanded, click the Info tab to open the Info panel.

If the panel group is collapsed, double-click the Info tab or click to the right of the tabs to open the Info panel.

3 Choose View > Rulers to turn on rulers along the left and top of the Stage.

4 Click and drag down a guide from the horizontal (top) ruler. Watch the Info panel; when the cursor location's y value is 75, release the mouse. Drag out two more rules at 95 and 475.

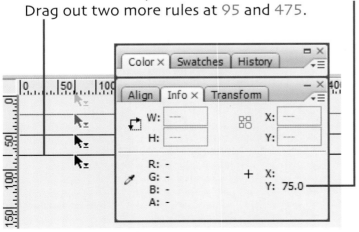

5 Make sure that Snap to Guides is turned on. Choose View > Snapping. In the drop-down menu, look for a check mark next to Snap to Guides. If there's no check mark, click Snap to Guides to turn it on.

design the layout of your stage

draw background

With our Stage divided into different areas, we're ready to begin drawing the objects that will serve as the background for our Web site.

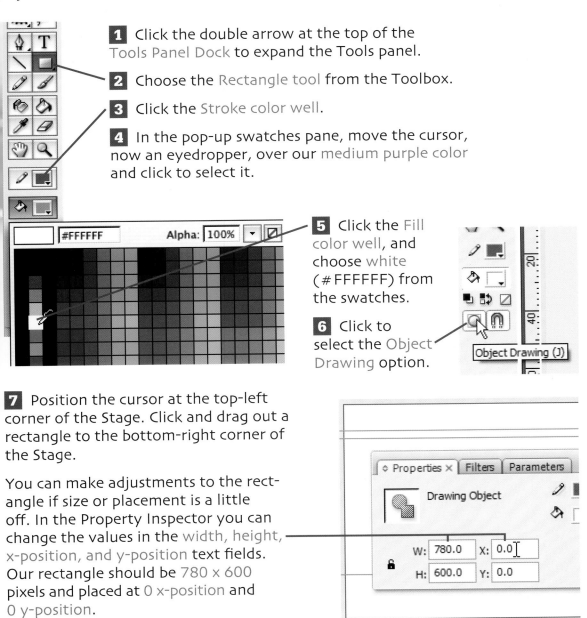

1 Click the double arrow at the top of the Tools Panel Dock to expand the Tools panel.

2 Choose the Rectangle tool from the Toolbox.

3 Click the Stroke color well.

4 In the pop-up swatches pane, move the cursor, now an eyedropper, over our medium purple color and click to select it.

5 Click the Fill color well, and choose white (#FFFFFF) from the swatches.

6 Click to select the Object Drawing option.

7 Position the cursor at the top-left corner of the Stage. Click and drag out a rectangle to the bottom-right corner of the Stage.

You can make adjustments to the rectangle if size or placement is a little off. In the Property Inspector you can change the values in the width, height, x-position, and y-position text fields. Our rectangle should be 780 x 600 pixels and placed at 0 x-position and 0 y-position.

design the layout of your stage　　　　　**11**

draw background (cont.)

For the next background element make sure the Rectangle tool is selected and the Object Drawing option is selected.

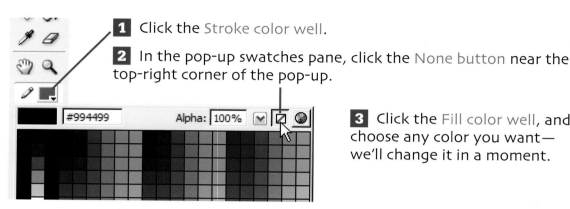

1 Click the Stroke color well.

2 In the pop-up swatches pane, click the None button near the top-right corner of the pop-up.

3 Click the Fill color well, and choose any color you want—we'll change it in a moment.

4 Position the cursor at the left edge of the Stage on top of the guide you placed at 75. Click and drag out a rectangle to the right edge of the Stage and down to the guide at 95.

If necessary, use the Property Inspector to set the dimension and position values to 780 X 20 and 0,75.

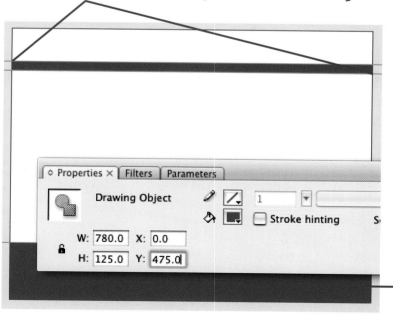

5 Draw another rectangle with these values: 780 X 125 and 0,475.

draw object primitives

Our final background element will be a special object known as a Rectangle Primitive. Primitive objects are special object shapes that allow you to adjust characteristics in the Property Inspector. This lets you precisely control the size, corner radius, and other properties of the shape at any time after you have created it without having to redraw it from scratch.

We'll use the corner radius feature of Rectangle Primitives to create a tabbed appearance in our layout.

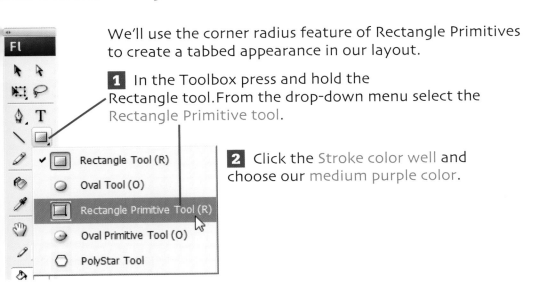

1 In the Toolbox press and hold the Rectangle tool. From the drop-down menu select the Rectangle Primitive tool.

2 Click the Stroke color well and choose our medium purple color.

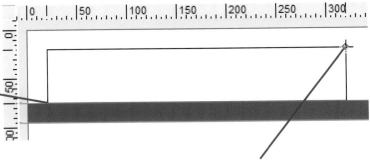

3 Position the cursor about 20 pixels from the left edge of the Stage on top of the guide you placed at 75.

4 Click and drag up and to the right. Release the mouse near the 20,320 position.

If necessary, use the Property Inspector to set the dimension and position values to 300 X 55 and 20,20.

edit primitives

Rectangle Primitive corners are changed by clicking and dragging the corner Radius Handles or by changing values in the Corner Radius controls in the Property Inspector. We'll do both.

1 Choose the Selection tool from the Toolbox.

2 Click one of the four Radius Handles on the Rectangle Primitive and drag either direction along the rectangle's edge. A guide appears showing the radius you are creating.

3 Release when you have a nicely rounded corner.

Note that all four corners of the Rectangle Primitive reflect the new radius you dragged out.

To create a tabbed appearance we only want rounded corners at the top left and right.

In the Property Inspector note that the value in the first Corner Radius control has changed and that the other three controls are disabled (grayed out).

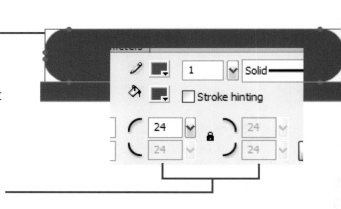

4 Click the Lock icon to unlock the relationship between the four corners, allowing each corner to be edited separately.

5 Change the bottom left and right values to 0 to bring them back to square corners.

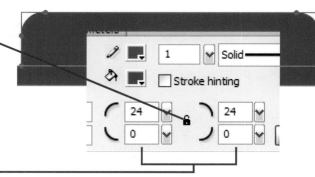

add gradient fills

Next we'll add gradient fills, in which colors gradually blend from one into another, to give our design a sense of depth.

Choose the Selection tool from the Toolbox, and click the rectangle between the guides at 75 and 95 to select it. Press [Shift] and click the rectangle you drew below the guide at 475 and the Rectangle Primitive to add them to the selection.

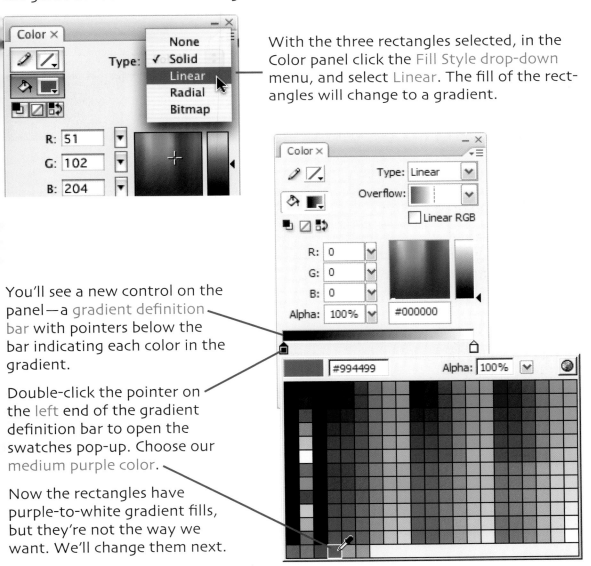

With the three rectangles selected, in the Color panel click the Fill Style drop-down menu, and select Linear. The fill of the rectangles will change to a gradient.

You'll see a new control on the panel—a gradient definition bar with pointers below the bar indicating each color in the gradient.

Double-click the pointer on the left end of the gradient definition bar to open the swatches pop-up. Choose our medium purple color.

Now the rectangles have purple-to-white gradient fills, but they're not the way we want. We'll change them next.

edit gradient fills

With the Selection tool, click outside the stage to deselect the three rectangles.

Select View > Guides > Show Guides to turn off guides, making our object edges easier to see.

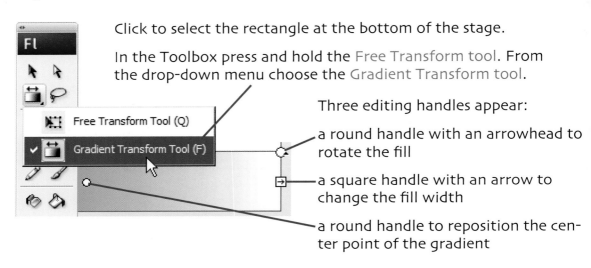

Click to select the rectangle at the bottom of the stage.

In the Toolbox press and hold the Free Transform tool. From the drop-down menu choose the Gradient Transform tool.

Three editing handles appear:

a round handle with an arrowhead to rotate the fill

a square handle with an arrow to change the fill width

a round handle to reposition the center point of the gradient

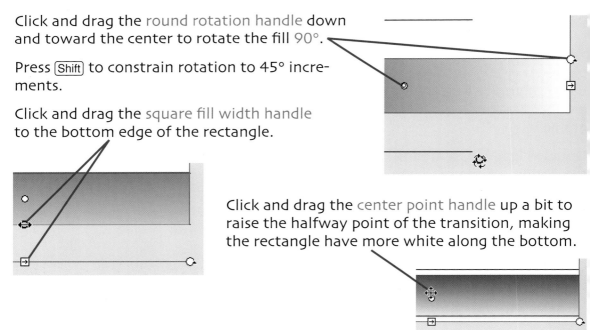

Click and drag the round rotation handle down and toward the center to rotate the fill 90°.

Press (Shift) to constrain rotation to 45° increments.

Click and drag the square fill width handle to the bottom edge of the rectangle.

Click and drag the center point handle up a bit to raise the halfway point of the transition, making the rectangle have more white along the bottom.

With the Gradient Transform tool
still selected, click to select the smaller
rectangle near the top of the Stage.

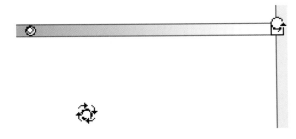

The three editing handles appear.

Rotate the fill 90°.

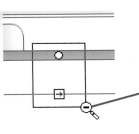

Zooming in on the rectangle and the gradient transform
handles will allow us to make more exact adjustments to the
gradient in the coming steps. Press and hold Ctrl Spacebar
(Windows) or ⌘ Spacebar (Mac) to temporarily change the
cursor to the Magnify tool. Click and drag out a rectangle
that surrounds the gradient center point and the square fill
width handle.

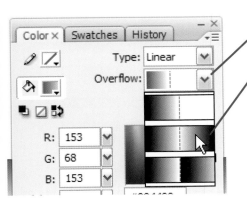

In the Color panel, click the Overflow
drop-down menu and choose the second
entry, which reflects a black-to-white-to-black
gradient. This makes the fill wrap to create
a 3D effect. Overflow defines how the fill
appears outside the boundaries of the gradient
fill width. Our selection reflects the gradient
across the fill width's edge.

Click and drag the square fill width handle
toward the center point until the two fill
guides are about halfway between the
center point and the edge of the rectangle.

Click and drag the center point handle
up a bit to raise the halfway point of the
transition, creating the 3D appearance.

design the layout of your stage

edit gradient fills (cont.)

Our final step in working with the gradient fills of the background objects is to apply and edit a Radial Gradient fill in the Rectangle Primitive.

Choose the Selection tool from the Toolbox and click to select the Rectangle Primitive with the tabbed appearance.

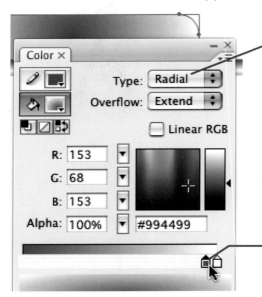

In the Color panel, click the Type drop-down menu (also referred to as Fill Style in the tool tip), and select Radial.

The fill changes to a Radial Gradient.

The gradient, with purple in the middle and white at the edges, is the opposite of what we want. We can redefine it in the Color panel.

On the gradient definition bar click and drag the purple-filled pointer to the right, stopping when you near the white pointer.

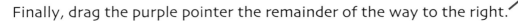

Now drag the white pointer to the left as far as it will go.

Finally, drag the purple pointer the remainder of the way to the right.

With the gradient colors set the way we want, we can modify the gradient appearance.

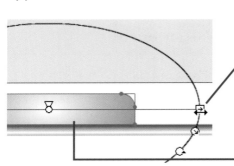

Select the Fill Transform tool.

Five editing handles appear, but we only need the square handle with an arrow that controls the fill width.

Click and drag the handle to the right, adjusting the fill so that more of the middle areas of the rectangle are near-white or light purple.

design the layout of your stage

3. add and style text

With the graphic elements of the background in place, we can now add some text. We begin by adding and manipulating static text. (In later chapters we'll do more advanced things with text.) In this chapter we'll do the following:

Add and manipulate fixed-width text boxes.

Apply universal modifications to a text box.

Add an e-mail link.

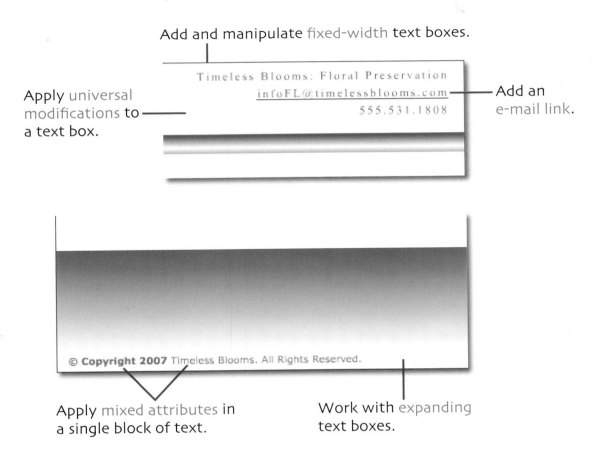

Apply mixed attributes in a single block of text.

Work with expanding text boxes.

add a single line of text

For our first simple text exercise we'll add company and copyright information to the layout.

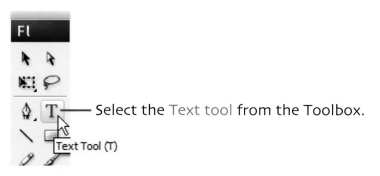

Select the Text tool from the Toolbox.

Text Tool (T)

In the Property Inspector, set attributes as follows:

Select Verdana for the Font.

Enter 10 for Font Size.

Click the Text (Fill) color control and choose our dark green color from the Color pop-up pane.

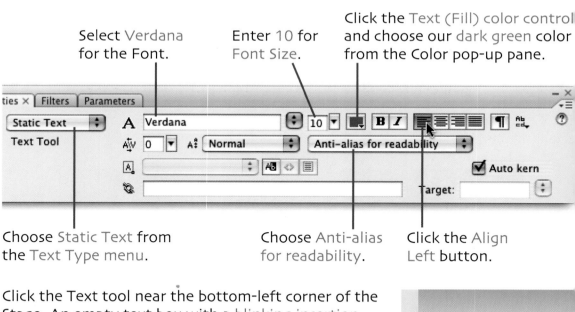

Choose Static Text from the Text Type menu.

Choose Anti-alias for readability.

Click the Align Left button.

Click the Text tool near the bottom-left corner of the Stage. An empty text box with a blinking insertion point appears. The round Resize handle denotes that the text box does not have a fixed width and will expand horizontally to hold all the text entered.

add and style text

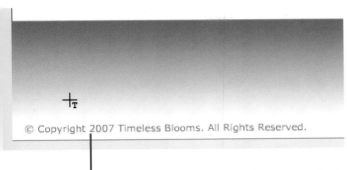

© Copyright 2007 Timeless Blooms. All Rights Reserved.

Type © Copyright 2007 Timeless Blooms. All Rights Reserved.

To enter the copyright symbol (©), press and hold [Option] and type [G] (Mac) or press and hold [Alt] and type 0169 on the number pad (Windows). (Note that you cannot enter the numbers from the main keyboard on Windows.)

Click on the Stage to close the text box.

Let's change the attributes of some of the text in this text box to add emphasis to the copyright notice.

With the Text tool still selected, click the text box to edit the text inside.

To select the text © Copyright 2007, click to the left of the copyright symbol and drag past the 7.

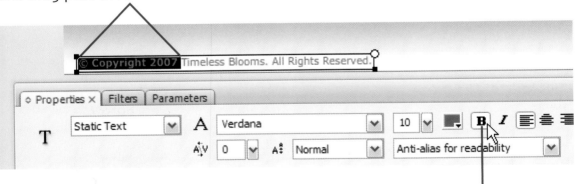

With the text now selected, click the Bold Style button in the Property Inspector.

fixed-width text

Click on the Stage to close and deselect the text box. In the Property Inspector, change the Font to Times New Roman and the Font Size to 12, and click to deselect the Bold Style button.

1 With the Text tool selected, move the cursor to a point near the top of the stage and aligned approximately with the 570 pixels mark on the horizontal ruler.

2 Click and drag out a text box, stopping near the 700 pixels mark.

An empty text box appears.

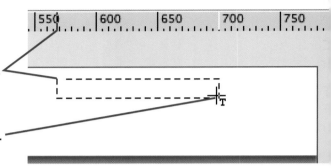

The square Resize handle denotes that the box has a fixed width, meaning text will wrap onto new lines rather than stay on one line and stretch the text box.

3 Enter Timeless Blooms: Floral Preservation.

Because the text box is not wide enough the last word will wrap to the next line.

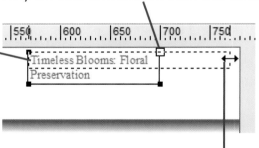

4 Click and drag the Resize handle to about the 770 pixels mark. Now the text fits on one line.

5 Press (←Enter), and type infoFL@timelessblooms.com.

6 Press (←Enter), and type 555.531.1808.

7 Choose the Selection tool from the Toolbox to close the text box.

add and style text

change a text box

You can make universal changes to all of the text in a text box by selecting the box and making changes in the Property Inspector.

If the text box is not still selected, click it with the Selection tool.

Click the Align Right button in the Property Inspector.

To spread out the lines of text, click the Edit Format Options button on the Property Inspector.

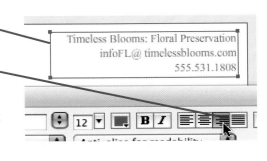

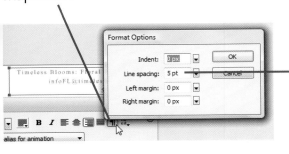

In the Format Options dialog, enter 5 for Line Spacing, and click OK.

Now let's spread the text out a bit. Enter 2 in the Property Inspector's Letter Spacing text field.

The last step caused the text on the first line to wrap again. Double-click the text box and drag out the Resize handle until the text fits on the first line again.

Now the text is drawing off the edge of the Stage! Move the cursor over the text container's bounding box until it changes to a pointer, and reposition the text box so that all the text appears on the Stage.

add an e-mail link

We want contacting Timeless Blooms to be convenient for viewers of the Web site. Let's add a link to the e-mail address that will automatically launch a new message in the viewer's e-mail application.

Double-click the text box to open it for editing. Select the text infoFL@timelessblooms.com.

Choose Edit > Copy to copy the e-mail address to the clipboard.

In the Property Inspector's URL Link field type mailto: and then paste the e-mail address into the field. Make sure there is no space between the colon and the pasted address.

Press ⏎Enter to set the URL attribute.

Standard convention on the Web is to underline clickable text. A dashed line appears under the e-mail address, but this is only a visual clue inside the Flash authoring environment; it won't be visible in the exported movie.

Flash doesn't provide an Underline style for text, so we'll create our own.

1 From the Toolbox, select the Line tool. Confirm that the Object Drawing option is selected.

2 In the Property Inspector, click the Stroke color well, and choose our dark purple color.

3 Enter 1 in the Stroke Height field.

4 Select Solid for the Stroke Style.

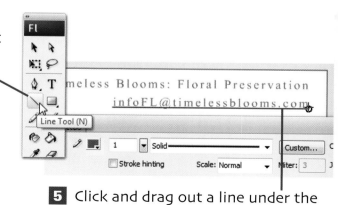

5 Click and drag out a line under the e-mail address.

4. work with imported objects

So far we've used Tools included in the Flash application to create different types of objects for our layout. In this chapter, we learn how to incorporate layout elements created in other graphics applications.

We'll also learn to keep the elements in our project organized, allowing for increased ease of development tasks. We'll learn to:

Import and transform vector artwork.

Apply transformations to objects.

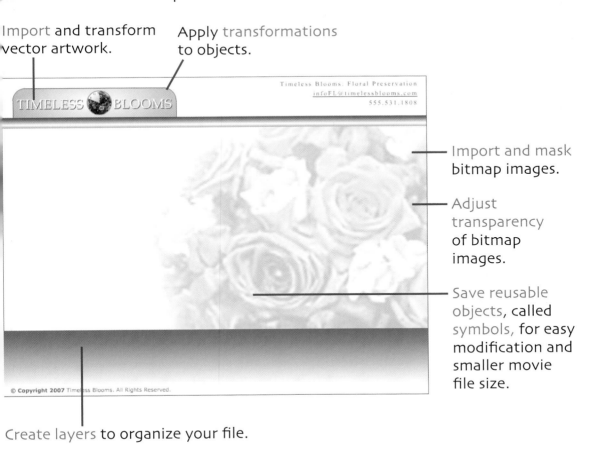

Import and mask bitmap images.

Adjust transparency of bitmap images.

Save reusable objects, called symbols, for easy modification and smaller movie file size.

Create layers to organize your file.

reusable graphics

Since the framework that we've created will
serve as the background of our Web site, we
can reuse what we've drawn multiple times,
for each page of our site. To do that, we
need to convert the elements into one reusable symbol. When a symbol is used on the
Stage, it's called an instance. (See extra bits
on Page 38.)

To select all the elements of the framework,
choose Edit > Select All, or press Ctrl A
(Windows) or ⌘A (Mac).

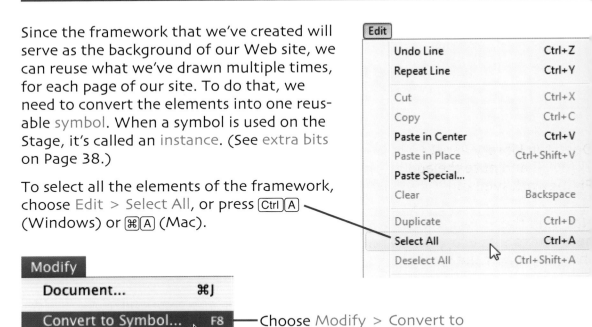

Choose Modify > Convert to
Symbol, or press F8 .

In the Convert to Symbol dialog,
name the symbol Framework.

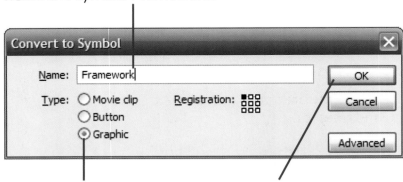

Select Graphic as the Type, and click OK.

The rectangles and text that we created so far have now
been moved into the Framework symbol, and an instance
of that symbol has replaced them on the Stage.

work with imported objects

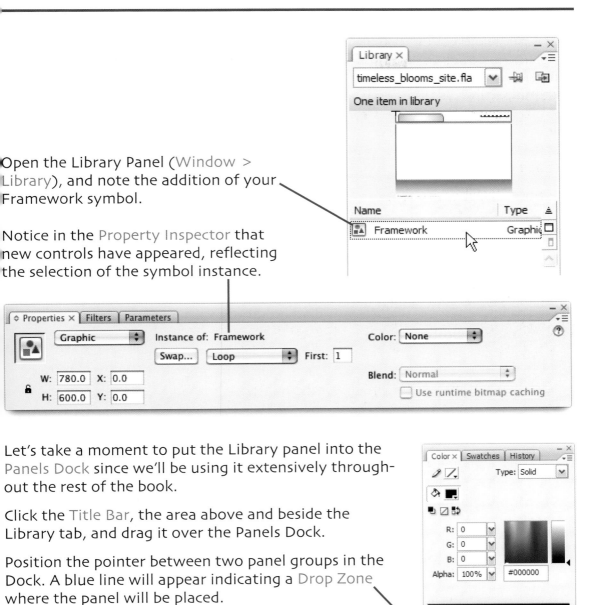

Open the Library Panel (Window > Library), and note the addition of your Framework symbol.

Notice in the Property Inspector that new controls have appeared, reflecting the selection of the symbol instance.

Let's take a moment to put the Library panel into the Panels Dock since we'll be using it extensively throughout the rest of the book.

Click the Title Bar, the area above and beside the Library tab, and drag it over the Panels Dock.

Position the pointer between two panel groups in the Dock. A blue line will appear indicating a Drop Zone where the panel will be placed.

Release the panel.

work with imported objects

import vector art

Sometimes you'll need to include artwork that has been created in another application or file format. Here we're going to import logo artwork that's been provided in an Adobe Fireworks PNG file that contains vectors (editable paths) and bitmap objects (images).

Choose File > Import > Import to Library to insert the logo file into your movie as a symbol.

In the Import to Library dialog, locate the file logo.png, which you downloaded from this book's companion Web site and copied into the site's development_files folder. Select the file, and click Open (Windows) or Import to Library (Mac).

In the Import Fireworks Document dialog that appears, set the following options:

Objects: Keep all paths editable

Text: Either choice will work in this case because all the text in the logo has been converted to vector paths to avoid font issues.

Do not check the Import as a single flattened bitmap check box.

Import: Page

Into: Current frame as movie clip

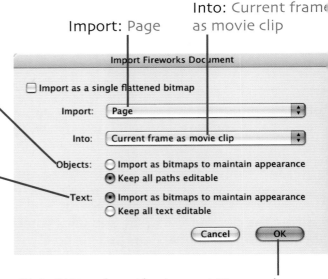

Click OK to close the Import Fireworks Document dialog.

Now the logo has been added to the Library

work with imported objects

organize symbols

In the Library panel, you'll see two new listings—a graphic symbol named logo.png and a folder named Fireworks Objects that contains the objects that make up the logo. Let's take a moment to begin organizing our symbols, which will save us time and headaches later.

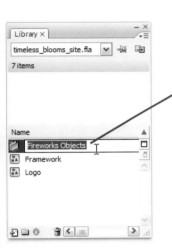

Double-click the symbol name logo.png in the Library panel to select the text. Change it to Logo, and press ←Enter.

Double-click the folder name to select the text Fireworks Objects. Enter T_Blooms Logo, and press ←Enter.

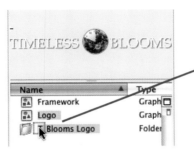

Click to select the symbol Logo, and drag the symbol onto the T_Blooms Logo folder.

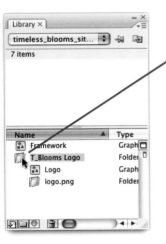

Double-click the T_Blooms Logo folder icon to expand the folder view, and verify that the symbol is in the folder along with the folders containing parts that make up the symbol Logo.

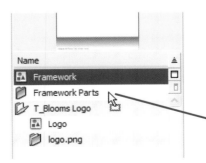

Click the New Folder button at the bottom of the Library panel to add a new folder to the list. Name the folder Framework Parts.

Drag the symbol Framework into the new folder.

symbol-editing mode

Once a symbol is created we'll often want to "get at" the elements inside for further editing. To do this we enter symbol-editing mode. (See extra bits on Page 38.) There are two styles of symbol-editing mode. Default Edit mode opens the symbol in its own window with no other elements visible. Edit in Place lets you edit the symbol in the location at which an instance is placed and allows you to see the other objects on the Stage.

There are also multiple ways to enter symbol-editing mode:

For default editing mode:

- Double-click the symbol preview or symbol icon in the Library panel.

- Select an instance on the Stage and choose Edit > Edit Symbols or Edit > Edit Selected.

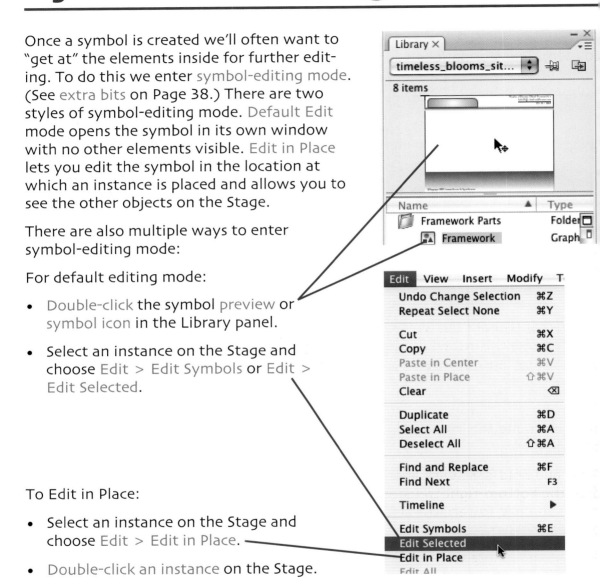

To Edit in Place:

- Select an instance on the Stage and choose Edit > Edit in Place.

- Double-click an instance on the Stage.

Edit in Place is our preferred manner because it allows you to edit the symbol in context with the rest of the Stage. When you're instructed to double-click a symbol or instance or to enter symbol-editing mode, always choose the Edit in Place mode, unless instructed otherwise.

Next, let's add a logo to the Framework symbol.

work with imported objects

transform objects

Objects on your Stage, even symbols, can have different transformations applied to them. Transformations such as Scale, Rotate, and Skew are applied with the Free Transform tool. (See extra bits on Page 38.)

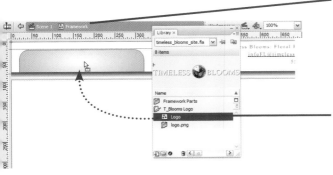

In the Edit Bar, confirm that you're still in symbol-editing mode on the symbol Framework. If not, double-click the instance on the Stage to invoke symbol-editing mode.

In the Library panel, click the symbol Logo, and drag it onto the Stage over the Rectangle Primitive.

The logo is bigger than we need, so we'll scale the instance down. With the instance still selected, choose the Free Transform tool.

Eight transformation handles appear around the instance's bounding box.

Press and hold (Shift). Click and drag the bottom-right transformation handle toward the center of the Logo symbol instance.

Release the mouse when all of the logo fits within the rectangle.

Use Arrow keys to nudge the logo into centered position over the Rectangle Primitive.

Choose the Selection tool to set the transformation.

object hierarchies

We use various constructs like Scenes, Frames, Layers, Symbols, and Groups as containers to organize files. Editing symbols and groups can get confusing because often times groups are placed inside other groups that are inside symbols inside other symbols. Confused yet? Imagine what it's like to edit them! The keys to success are the Edit Bar and the Property Inspector. Let's try it.

In the Edit Bar confirm you're still in symbol-editing mode on the Framework symbol. Select the Logo instance and choose View > Magnification > 400% to zoom way in.

1 Double-click on the clock. The Edit Bar shows you're editing 3 levels in—Scene 1 > Framework > Logo.

2 Click to select the clock. The Property Inspector shows that an instance of symbol Page is selected.

3 Double-click the clock again. The Edit Bar shows you're one level further in.

4 Select the clock again. The Property Inspector shows the clock is actually a group.

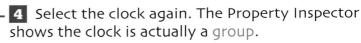

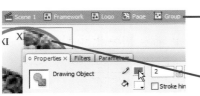

5 Double-click the clock group. The Edit Bar reflects the new editing level, Scene 1 > Framework > Logo > Page > Group.

6 Finally, we can select the object we want, a circle with a purple stroke that makes up the clock's frame. To select it, zoom to 800% and click on the very edge of the purple frame. It might take a couple of tries to select the circle and not the bouquet image.

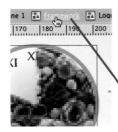

7 Once selected, click the Stroke color well in the Property Inspector and choose our orange color.

With the edit made we can return to editing the Framework symbol by clicking Framework in the Edit Bar.

work with imported objects

organize with layers

Layers, as we outlined before, are a great organizational tool. They control the stacking order of objects in a Timeline. We're going to create a new layer above the current one and move our logo there. But first let's modify our workspace.

We're going to be working away from the panels in the Panel Dock for a bit, so let's take this opportunity to maximize our work area by collapsing the Panels Dock to the Icons and Text configuration.

Click the double arrow at the top of the Panels Dock to collapse it.

Now let's begin working with layers. We're going to rename the current layer to reflect what it contains.

If the Timeline isn't already visible, click the Show/Hide Timeline button in the Edit Bar or choose Window > Timeline.

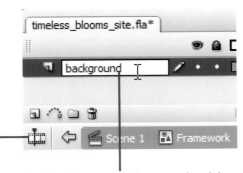

In the Layers column, double-click the text Layer 1 to select it. Enter background for the layer name, and press ←Enter.

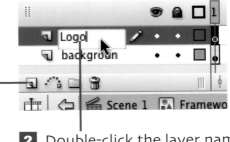

1 Click the Insert Layer button at the bottom of the Layers column. A new layer appears in the layers list.

2 Double-click the layer name, and change it to Logo.

move between layers

Now we want to move the symbol Logo from the background layer to the new layer that we've created to hold it. Moving objects from one layer to another in Flash works differently than in most drawing applications. Here's how it's done.

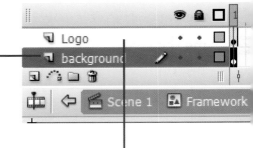

With the Selection tool, click to select the instance of the symbol Logo on the background layer.

Choose Edit > Cut to move the Logo instance from the background layer to the clipboard.

In the Timeline, click the Logo layer to make it the active layer.

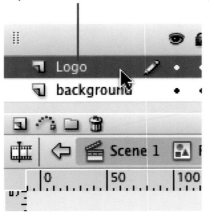

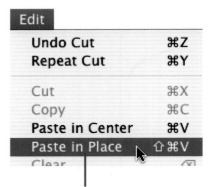

Choose Edit > Paste in Place to paste the Logo instance into the exact same location, just on the different layer.

work with imported objects

import bitmap image

With the logo sized and placed, we're going to add some interest to the main area of our layout.

In the Edit Bar confirm that you are still in symbol-editing mode.

1 In the Timeline, add a new layer to your Framework symbol.

2 Name the layer bouquet.

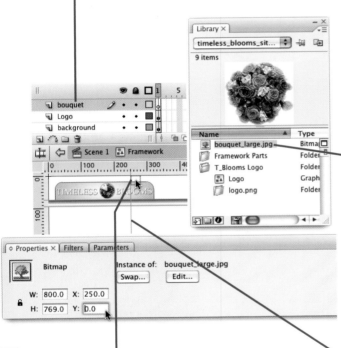

3 In the Panels Dock, click the Library icon to open the panel.

4 Choose File > Import > Import to Library. In the Import dialog, navigate to the development_files folder. Select the bouquet_large.jpg file, and click Open.

The bouquet image is placed in the Library.

5 We'll use the guides we placed earlier and add a new one to help position the image. Choose View > Guide > Show Guides to turn them on.

6 On Windows, click the bouquet_large.jpg symbol and drag it onto the Stage, aligning the left edge with the vertical guide and the top edge with the top of the Stage.

On Mac, click the bouquet_large.jpg symbol. Drag and drop it anywhere on the Stage. Use the Property Inspector to set the position to x = 250 and y = 0.

From the vertical ruler drag out a guide and place it approximately halfway between the bouquet/clock in the logo and the right edge of the Rectangle Primitive.

work with imported objects

add masking layer

The bouquet image is too big and covers up too much of the layout. We only want part of the bouquet image to display, so we'll use a Layer Mask to hide the unwanted parts.

1 In the Timeline, click in the Eye column to the right of the layer name bouquet to temporarily hide the image.

2 Add a new layer, and name it bouquet mask.

3 Select the Rectangle tool.

4 Set the Stroke color well to none.

5 Set the Fill color well to black.

6 Place the cursor over the intersection of the horizontal guide at 95 and the vertical guide aligned with the left edge of the image.

7 Click and drag down and to the right to the guide at 475 and the right edge of the stage.

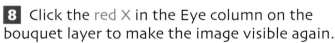

8 Click the red X in the Eye column on the bouquet layer to make the image visible again.

9 Right-click (Windows) or Control-click (Mac) the layer bouquet_mask. Choose Mask from the drop-down menu.

Note that the bouquet and bouquet_mask layers are locked. This is required for the mask to display correctly.

The visible areas of the image are now cropped within the confines of the masking rectangle.

work with imported objects

edit masked objects

Finally, for the layout we want to fade the bouquet image so that it is very light behind the content we'll be adding later.

To edit a masked object, you must temporarily turn the masking off by unlocking the two layers that make up the mask.

1 In the Timeline, click the Lock icons in the bouquet_mask and bouquet layers.

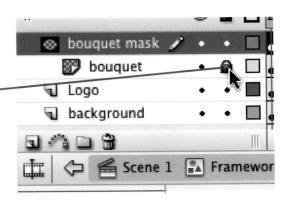

The full bouquet image and the black rectangle are now visible on the Stage.

To adjust transparency, called Alpha, of an object, it must be converted to a symbol.

2 Click to select the bouquet image.

3 Choose Modify > Convert to Symbol, or press F8. In the Convert to Symbol dialog, name the symbol Masked Bouquet. Select Graphic as the Type, and click OK.

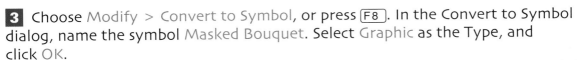

4 In the Property Inspector, click the Color Styles menu, and select Alpha. Set the Alpha Amount to 20%.

The bitmap image is faded the way we want.

5 To turn masking back on, click in the Lock column of the bouquet_mask and bouquet layers.

In the Edit Bar click Scene 1 to exit symbol-editing mode.

That's it! Our layout framework is now complete.

extra bits

reusable graphics p. 26

- Using symbols in Flash provides two main benefits: reduced file size and ease of editing.

  When you create a symbol and place instances of that symbol on the Stage, your movie's file size is reduced because no matter how many times you use it, the code required to define it is only included in the file once. Each instance just points to the symbol and describes any modifications to that symbol, such as transparency or size.

  Modifying work later is also much easier. Imagine that you've placed 100 blue squares (not instances of a blue square symbol) throughout your movie, and then you decide to change the color. You have to find and change all 100 squares. But if you made a symbol of a blue square and placed 100 instances, you only have to change the symbol, and the 100 instances are updated automatically.

symbol-editing mode p. 30

- When you have an object on the Stage that is a container for other objects (groups, symbols and text boxes), you can just double-click it to "get inside" and edit the contents.

- To exit the editing mode of the container, you can double-click outside the bounds of the container.

transform objects p. 31

- When you're scaling vector objects (those drawn in Flash or imported from Illustrator or Fireworks, as in the logo file) you can increase or decrease the size without negative effect. However, if you're working with a bitmap image, you'll want to avoid enlarging it. An enlarged bitmap has to be resampled and can become distorted or fuzzy. It's best to open the image in an image editor such as Adobe Photoshop and scale it to the size you need.

5. use the timeline to organize your site

As you've probably guessed, the Timeline is used for animation in your Flash movie. But it also serves other purposes.

A frame can represent not only a fluid moment in an animation as an object slides across the Stage, but also a static point to which we navigate within our movie. In Flash development we use frames for animation, as reference points, and as organizational tools to ease development.

In this chapter, we learn the basics of working with different types of frames, naming frames for easy reference, and controlling frame playback. We'll learn to:

Add frame labels   Insert keyframes

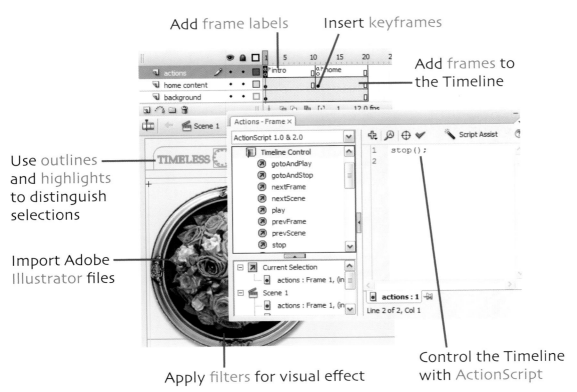

Add frames to the Timeline

Use outlines and highlights to distinguish selections

Import Adobe Illustrator files

Apply filters for visual effect

Control the Timeline with ActionScript

illustrator import

We've established the framework for our design. Now it's time to work on the Home section of the site. First, let's add some content from an Adobe Illustrator file. Flash offers many options for importing layers and objects in the file, and we'll make selections based on how we'll use the different elements in our project.

Turn off guides by selecting View > Guides > Show Guides or pressing [Ctrl][;] (Windows) or [⌘][;] (Mac).

1 In the Timeline, rename the existing layer background.

2 Add a new layer and leave the default name Layer 2; it will be changed later.

3 Add another layer named actions.

4 Click Layer 2; to make it the active layer.

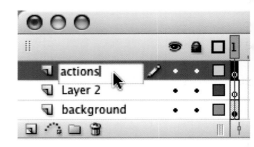

5 Choose File > Import > Import to Stage. In the Import dialog, navigate to the development_files folder. Select the file T_Blooms Home Content.ai, and click Open.

The Import "T_Blooms Home Content.ai" to Stage dialog that appears provides import options that we can customize.

The Object Options section of the dialog displays all of the different layers and objects that are in the Illustrator file.

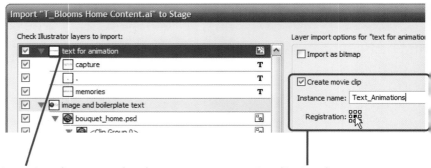

Select the text for animation layer and select Create movie clip in the Layer Import Options section of the dialog. Enter Instance Name Text_Animations. In the Registration control, click the center square. The layer contains three text blocks to be used in an animation. Importing them into a Movie Clip will save us time later.

Set the three text objects to import as: Editable Text.

Select the layer image and boilerplate text. Choose Create Movie Clip and name it Image_and_Text.

Select bouquet_home.psd and choose Import as Bitmap to collapse the sub-items into one image.

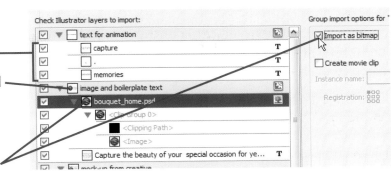

Set the line of text that begins "Capture the beauty of..." to Import as Vector Outlines.

Uncheck the box next to the layer mock-up from creative so it won't be imported.

Set Convert Layers to Single Flash Layer.

Uncheck the remaining options, and click OK.

With the Selection tool, drag the graphics into place.

The layer name has changed to match the file name we imported. Change it to home content.

In the Library panel, a folder named T_Blooms Home Content.ai is created. Rename the folder Home Parts.

As a clean-up action, drag bouquet_ large.jpg and Masked Bouquet into the Framework Parts folder.

I won't instruct you to organize symbols throughout the rest of this book; however, keep in mind the techniques covered earlier.

outlines & highlights

You may have noticed that it is sometimes difficult to identify what objects you have selected or that it is difficult to examine an object because of the surrounding objects. There are two related features, Outline Display and Colored Highlights, that address those difficulties.

In the Layers Column of the Timeline, clicking the color icons at the right turns the objects in that layer to Outline Display.

In the layer background click the green icon.

Note that the objects in the framework now display as outlines and the outline color matches the color of the icon for that layer.

Click the icon again to turn Outline Display off.

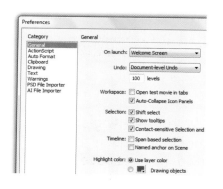

You can also use the colors for Outline Mode to highlight selected objects.

Choose Edit > Preferences (Windows) or Flash > Preferences (Mac) to open the Preferences dialog.

In the Category List, select General.

Change the Highlight Color setting to Use layer color.

Click OK.

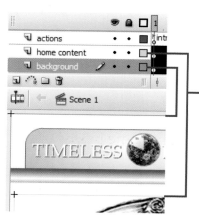

Shift-click the bouquet image and the Framework symbol to select them both.

Note that the highlight color for the bouquet image matches the color in the home content layer and the highlight color on the background symbol matches the background layer.

add a drop shadow

We'd like a bit more visual punch with our content graphics. We'll add a Drop Shadow Filter to the framed bouquet image to help achieve that. Launch symbol-editing mode for the image and boilerplate text symbol.

Click the Stage outside the bounding boxes of the image and text to deselect them. Click to select the framed bouquet image.

In the Property Inspector select the Filters tab. The Property Inspector shows that filters are only applied to text, movie clips, and buttons, so we'll need to convert our selection to a symbol.

Choose Modify > Convert to Symbol. In the dialog name it Framed Bouquet, choose Movie Clip type, and click OK.

With the symbol now selected, click the Add Filter button on the Filters tab, and choose Drop Shadow from the drop-down menu.

New controls for manipulating the shadow appear on the tab. Choose these settings:

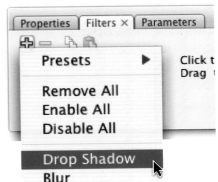

Strength: 40%   Blur: 10   Color: Black

Angle: 75

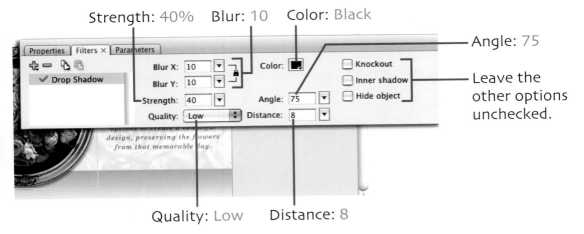

Leave the other options unchecked.

Quality: Low   Distance: 8

Exit symbol-editing mode by double-clicking outside the bounding box of the image or choose Scene 1 in the Edit Bar.

Now the image has a nice drop shadow effect that adds visual depth to the layout.

frames & keyframes

Currently we have only one frame in our movie. The frames that you see in the Timeline now are available frames, but they're not yet defined. We'll define more frames to help us organize our movie and prepare it for adding animations (which we'll do in the next chapter). (See extra bits on Page 49.)

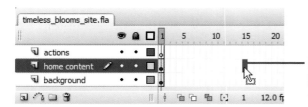

In the Timeline for the home content layer, click the empty cell beneath the 15 marker in the Timeline Header.

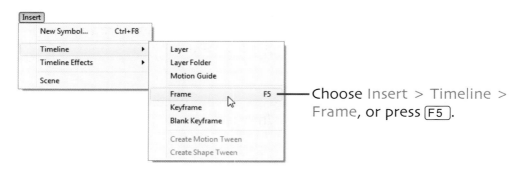

Choose Insert > Timeline > Frame, or press F5.

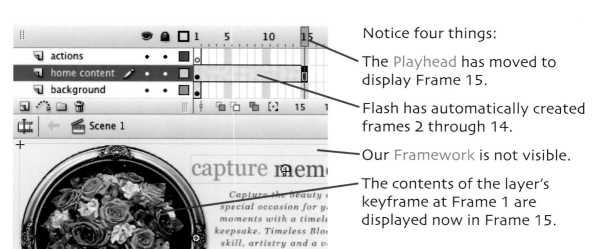

Notice four things:

The Playhead has moved to display Frame 15.

Flash has automatically created frames 2 through 14.

Our Framework is not visible.

The contents of the layer's keyframe at Frame 1 are displayed now in Frame 15.

use the timeline to organize your site

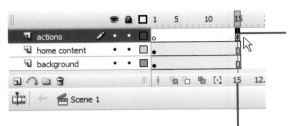

We have no Framework because Frame 15 has not been defined for the background layer. Add the frame now, repeating the steps you took to create the frame for the home content layer.

Insert Frame 15 for the actions layer.

Note the Current Frame display beneath the Timeline in case you have difficulty determining what frame you're in.

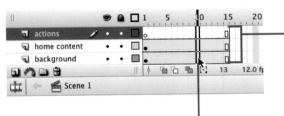

We now have 15 frames in each of our layers. Let's add five more frames to all the layers at once.

In the actions layer, click one of the frames and drag down to the background layer, selecting the frame in all three layers. Choose Insert > Timeline > Frame five times, or press F5 five times.

Now we're going to add keyframes, which will let us change content from one point in the Timeline to another.

Click Frame 11 in the home content layer, and choose Insert > Timeline > Keyframe.

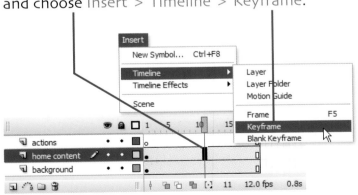

We do this because later we're going to add a text animation that plays when our movie first loads. Keyframe 1 will contain the text animation, and Keyframe 11 will contain static text.

use the timeline to organize your site

add frame labels

Frame labels let you name frames for logical reference. (See extra bits on Page 49.)

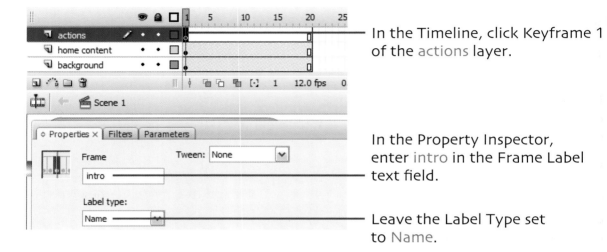

In the Timeline, click Keyframe 1 of the actions layer.

In the Property Inspector, enter intro in the Frame Label text field.

Leave the Label Type set to Name.

Note that Keyframe 1 in the Timeline now displays a flag signifying that it has a label. Also, because this keyframe has a span of several more frames, Flash has room to display the frame label in the Timeline.

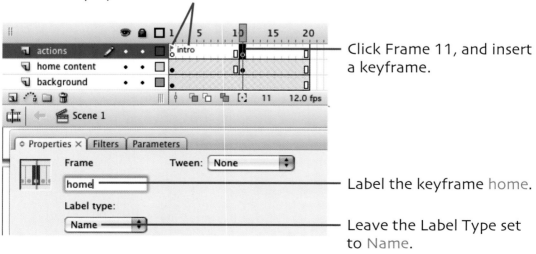

Click Frame 11, and insert a keyframe.

Label the keyframe home.

Leave the Label Type set to Name.

use the timeline to organize your site

control the timeline

By default, the Playhead in a Flash movie plays through all the frames in a Timeline and loops endlessly unless you tell it otherwise. We use Actions applied to frames and buttons to control the Playhead. (See extra bits on Page 50.)

We'll stop the Playhead in keyframe intro by adding a Stop action.

Click Keyframe intro in the actions layer.

In the Panels Dock, click the Actions icon to open the Actions panel.

Confirm that ActionScript 1.0 & 2.0 is selected in the Actions Filter drop-down menu at the top of the Actions Toolbox.

In the Actions Toolbox, click Global Functions to open the functions list.

Click Timeline Control.

Locate the stop function.

Double-click stop.

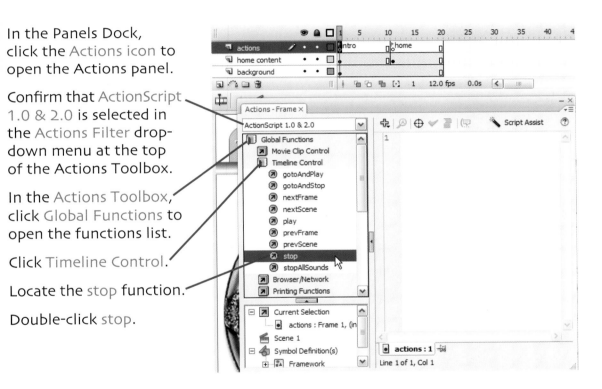

control the timeline (cont.)

Note two things:

In the Timeline, an a is displayed in the keyframe, signifying that this frame has ActionScript applied to it.

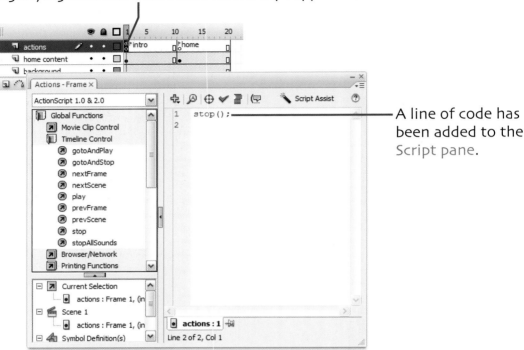

A line of code has been added to the Script pane.

Congratulations! You've just used ActionScript to control your movie!

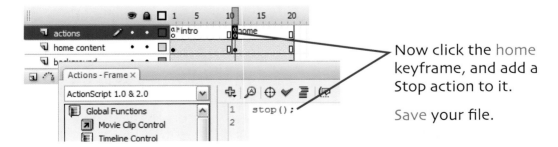

Now click the home keyframe, and add a Stop action to it.

Save your file.

use the timeline to organize your site

extra bits

frames & keyframes p. 44

- Every Flash movie contains multiple Timelines. Every scene has a main Timeline, and each symbol has its own independent Timeline, as you saw when editing the Framework symbol.

  Within a scene or symbol, each layer also has its own Timeline. In complex Flash movies like the one we're building, it is best to use the scene's main Timeline for organizational and reference purposes only. Use the Timelines available inside symbols for animation.

- We define two kinds of frames in a Timeline—basic frames and keyframes. Keyframes are where we do all of our work. Whenever you want to manually change the contents of a frame, you must do it in a keyframe. Basic frames make up what is known as a keyframe's span—the frames between that keyframe and the next. Frames act merely as clones of the preceding keyframe.

- By default, the first frame in any Timeline is a keyframe.

- If you change an object in a frame, you're actually making that change to the keyframe and all frames in its span. It can be incredibly painful to make a change in a particular frame, thinking that you're only changing

that frame, and 30 minutes later realize you actually changed 15 frames, so be careful that you are always editing in a keyframe.

- In the Timeline, keyframes are marked with a bullet. A solid bullet signifies that the keyframe has contents, and a hollow bullet signifies an empty keyframe. The final frame in a keyframe span is marked with a hollow rectangle.

add frame labels p. 46

- When you're working with multiple Timelines throughout your movie, moving objects from place to place, and adding or removing frames as you work, it can be difficult to remember what frame number holds an object you're looking for or want to link to from elsewhere in the movie.

  If you have objects on a keyframe at Frame 70 but then add 8 frames to the Timeline, your keyframe is now at 78. If buttons or other movie clips are linking to that keyframe by number, you have to remember to search them out and change the link from 70 to 78. But if you've labeled the keyframe important_frame, that doesn't change, and all the pointers in your movie that point to important_frame are still correct.

continues on next page

use the timeline to organize your site

- It's a common practice in Flash development to add frames after a keyframe just to make enough room to display the frame label, making it easy to locate frames during development. In our Timeline so far, the only frames that will actually be seen by viewers are frames 1 and 11; the other frames will be bypassed. You'll understand this more when we add animations and navigation controlled with ActionScript later in the book.

control the timeline p. 47

- To help keep us organized, we add an empty layer named actions to each of our Timelines—using the layer only for labeling and Action-Script. This helps us keep the mechanics of our movie separate from the content and lets us visually track frame properties easily.

- ActionScript is Flash's powerful scripting language that allows developers to control playback and establish complex interactions. While it is considered an easy language to use, those of us who are not programmers don't necessarily think so.

Flash does provide some features, like Script Assist mode, that help novices develop scripts, but even using Script Assist effectively requires some understanding of what's going on.

Throughout the book we'll both create some ActionScript on our own to learn some basics and use the Script Assist feature to get us over some of the hurdles.

Flash CS3 Professional introduces a new version of the ActionScript programming language know as ActionScript 3 (AS3). The primary target of AS3 is programmers who are doing complex application development in Flash and in Adobe Flex—Flash's application development sister application. The complexity of AS3 and the programming knowledge required to use it are well beyond our scope.

The Timeline-based actions that we execute in our site, like animations, Timeline control, and loading static external content, are better suited to ActionScript 2, so that's what we've chosen to use.

6. add animation to your web site

By now you might be thinking "Enough with the boring stuff. I want to make things fly across the Stage." If that's the case, then you're going to love this chapter. Here we add the pizzazz to our Web site that separates it from an ordinary HTML-based site. In the following pages we'll do these tasks:

Add a Transition effect to make the bouquet image and text fade-in slowly

Use ActionScript to pause playback and play animations at just the right moment

Tween a Filter Effect to enhance an animation

Use Timeline Effects to build a complex animation where text zooms in and out, changing words as it goes

create a tween

The first piece of the animated intro we'll create in this chapter will slide part of our text into place from off Stage. To create the animation, we set up our content's beginning state and ending state, and then instruct Flash to create, or tween, the intermediate frames. (See extra bits on Page 73.)

In the Timeline, click keyframe intro of layer home content to select all of its contents—the two symbol instances. We'll use the symbols in the intro animation, so we want to put them in a Movie Clip symbol.

Choose Modify > Convert to Symbol, or press F8.

In the Convert to Symbol dialog, name the symbol Intro Animation, choose Movie Clip as the Type, and select the top-left Registration point. Click OK.

In the Property Inspector name the instance introAnimation.

Double-click the new instance to invoke symbol-editing mode.

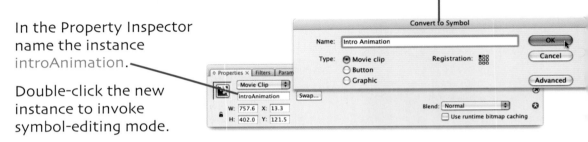

Double-click the text for animation symbol instance that contains the text "capture memories" in order to edit it.

There are three text pieces: capture, memories, and a period (.), that we want to move to individual layers.

If they're not selected, select the three pieces of text.

Right-click (Windows) or Control-click (Mac), and choose Distribute to Layers from the drop-down menu.

In the Timeline, three new layers are created. The original layer remains but is empty. Rename the layer actions.

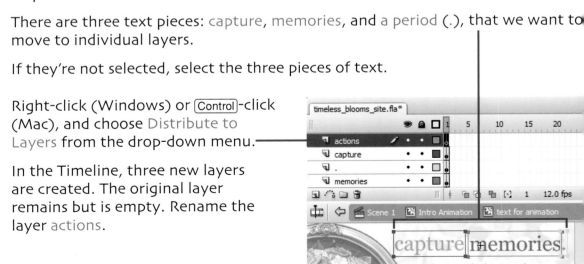

add animation to your web site

Change the name of Layer "." to period.

Click Frame 40 in layer capture and drag down to select the frame in layer period. Insert a keyframe ([F6]).

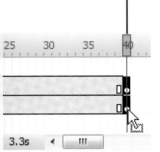

Move the Playhead back to Frame 1.

With the Selection tool, select capture and the period (.).

Press [Shift] and drag the text to the left until the period is just off the edge of the Stage.

Click away from the text to deselect it.

In the Timeline, click Frame 1 of layer capture and drag down to select the frame in the layer period.

In the Property Inspector, click the Tween Type drop-down menu (labeled Tween), and choose Motion.

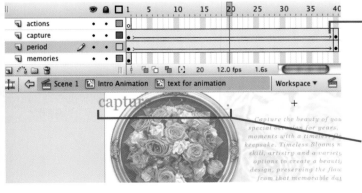

Notice in the Timeline that an arrow is displayed from Keyframe 1 to Keyframe 40 in both layers, signifying applied tweens.

Move the Playhead to a couple of different frames between 1 and 40 and notice the incremental changes in position.

That's it. You just created your first tweened animation.

add animation to your web site 53

play animation in flash

You can preview an animation inside the Flash application. Let's watch the animation we just created. Choose Control > Play, or press ←Enter.

You may think the animation is a bit choppy. This happens when there are too many frames in an animation and the eye is able to distinguish too many of the individual static images. Let's shorten the animation to make that less noticeable.

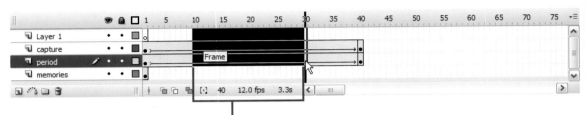

In the Timeline, click a frame and drag down and to the right—selecting approximately 20 frames in each of the two layers. Be sure you don't drag past Frame 39, selecting the keyframe.

Choose Edit > Timeline > Remove Frames, or press Shift F5. The animation is shortened, and Flash re-interpolates the tweened frames.

Press ←Enter to view the animation now.

You should see an appreciably smoother animation.

tween filter effects

To further enhance the animation, let's blur the text as it slides in to give the appearance of a motion trail. We'll add a Blur filter and have Flash tween it.

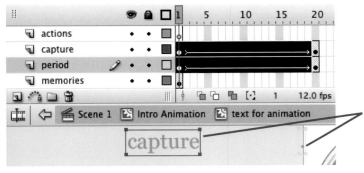

Move the Playhead back to Frame 1.

Scroll your document window until capture is visible.

Select capture and ".".

Select the Filters tab in the Property Inspector.

Add a Blur filter from the Add Filter drop-down menu.

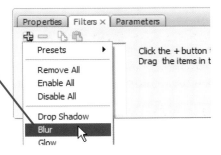

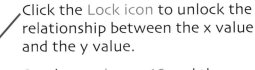

Click the Lock icon to unlock the relationship between the x value and the y value.

Set the x value at 40 and the y value at 0 to blur only left and right.

Move the Playhead to the final frame in the tween. Note that there is no blur on the text.

Move the Playhead to several frames between the final frame and Frame 1.

Note the varying degrees of blur.

Press ⏎Enter to view the animation now.

add animation to your web site

add timeline effects

As easy as creating the tweened animation was, Flash goes one major step further. Timeline Effects allow quick and easy creation of some of the most common, but more complex, animation techniques developers want to create.

For the next piece of our intro, we'll use a series of Timeline Effects to create an animation in which text zooms in and out, changing from capture moments. to capture memories..

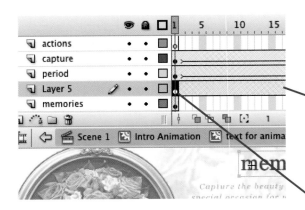

In Keyframe 1, select memories.

Choose Edit > Copy to copy the text to the clipboard.

Insert a new layer. Note that the new layer has Frames 1–20 already defined. That's because new layers match the number of frames used elsewhere in the Timeline.

Click Keyframe 1 in the new layer.

Choose Edit > Paste in Place.

With the Text tool, change the text to moments.

Note that moments is not visually as wide as memories underneath it. If we leave it this way, the spaces between moments and capture before it and the period after will be too big and will cause the text to look bad.

In the Toolbox, choose the Selection tool to select the text box.

In the Property Inspector, adjust Letter Spacing until the beginning letters (m) and ending letters (s) are closer to being aligned—about 2.

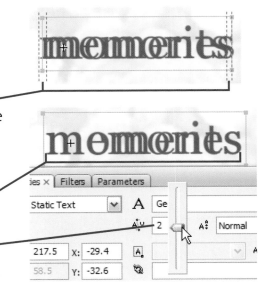

We'll need two animations of the word moments—one zooming in and one zooming out.

With moments selected, choose Edit > Copy to copy the text to the clipboard.

In the Timeline, insert a new layer.

Choose Edit > Paste in Place.

We now have moments on two layers.

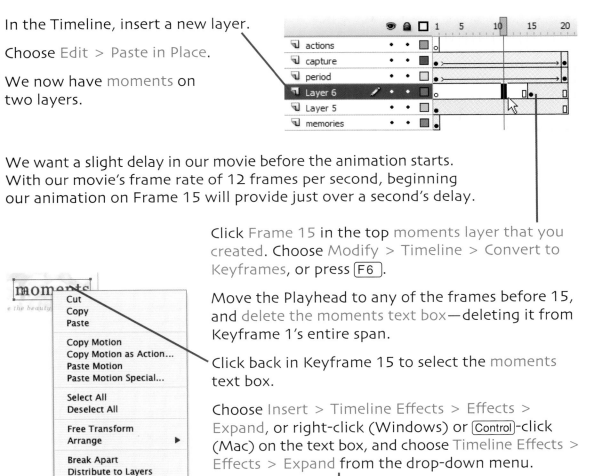

We want a slight delay in our movie before the animation starts. With our movie's frame rate of 12 frames per second, beginning our animation on Frame 15 will provide just over a second's delay.

Click Frame 15 in the top moments layer that you created. Choose Modify > Timeline > Convert to Keyframes, or press F6.

Move the Playhead to any of the frames before 15, and delete the moments text box—deleting it from Keyframe 1's entire span.

Click back in Keyframe 15 to select the moments text box.

Choose Insert > Timeline Effects > Effects > Expand, or right-click (Windows) or Control-click (Mac) on the text box, and choose Timeline Effects > Effects > Expand from the drop-down menu.

add animation to your web site   **57**

add timeline effects (cont.)

1 In the Expand dialog, select Squeeze for the Expand Style.

2 Click the Update Preview button, and note the change in the animation.

3 Enter 600 for the Fragment Offset value.

4 Set the values for Change Fragment Size by to 800 for Height and 400 for Width.

5 Click OK.

Press ⌐←Enter⌐ to preview the animation.

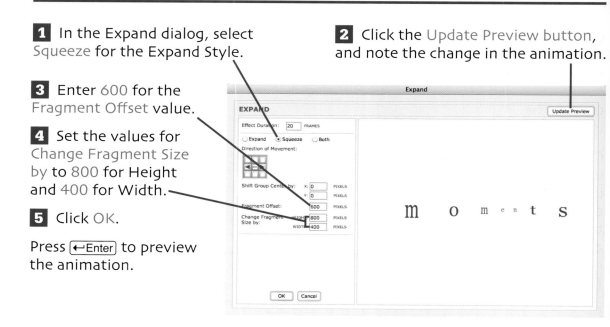

It's close to the effect we want, but the e is too far into the frame at the beginning and doesn't give the appearance that it has "flown in" from behind. We can fix that.

Move the Playhead back to Keyframe 15, and click the e to select the symbol that the effect created. (The original text box has been broken up into pieces; that's why we copied it into the other layer before we started adding the effect.)

In the Property Inspector, click the Edit button to launch the Expand dialog.

Confirm that the Expand Style is still set to Squeeze. (A bug in the initial release of Flash CS3 Professional resulted in the Expand Style setting changing to Both when editing an existing effect. This bug may have been fixed in subsequent updates.)

Change the Fragment Offset value to 800.

Click the Update Preview button, and note the change in the animation. You can even move the Expand dialog to reveal the Stage behind it and see that the e is now just outside the Stage in the first frame of the animation.

Click OK.

With our animation set to our liking, we're going to add a motion tween of alpha transparency.

Right-click Frame 34 in the layer containing the effect and choose Insert Keyframe from the drop-down menu. NOTE: Because of an "odd" behavior in Flash, you must use this method to insert the keyframe or this step won't work. Don't use the menu item Insert > Timeline > Keyframe or the shortcut key, F6.

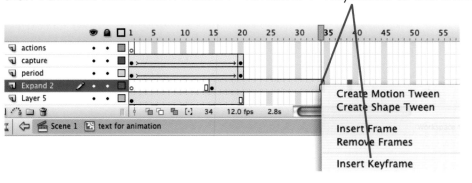

Read the warning dialog that appears, and click OK. We won't be able to make further changes in the Expand dialog.

add animation to your web site   **59**

add timeline effects (cont.)

Click Keyframe 15 in the layer containing the effect to select it.

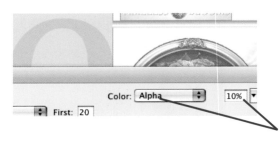

In the Property Inspector, click the Tween Type drop-down menu and choose Motion.

With the Selection tool, select the symbol by clicking on the e.

Click the Color Styles drop-down menu and select Alpha. Set the Alpha Amount to 10%.

Press ⏎Enter to preview the animation.

That completes the zoom-in of the text. Now let's do a reverse and zoom the text out.

Click Frame 35 in the next layer, which contains the remaining moments text box.

Insert a keyframe.

Move the Playhead to any of the frames before 35, and delete the moments text box—deleting it from Keyframe 1's entire span.

Click back in Keyframe 35 to select the moments text box.

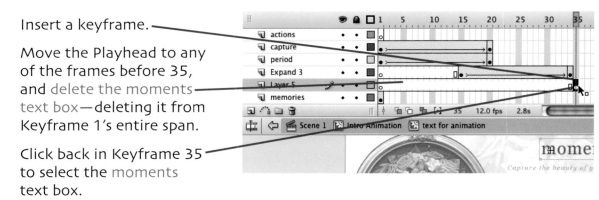

Choose Insert > Timeline Effects > Effects > Expand, or right-click (Windows) or Control-click (Mac) on the text box, and choose Timeline Effects > Effects > Expand from the drop-down menu.

In the Expand dialog, choose Expand as the Expand Style, enter 800 for the Fragment Offset, and set the values for Change Fragment Size by to 800 for Height and 400 for Width. Click OK.

In the Timeline, right-click Frame 54 in the layer containing the effect and choose Insert Keyframe from the drop-down menu. Again, note that you must use this method for inserting the keyframe.

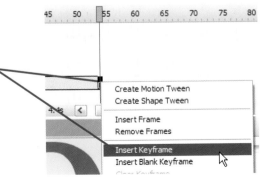

Read the warning dialog that appears, and click OK.

In Keyframe 54, click the e to select the symbol.

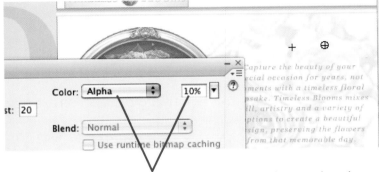

In the Property Inspector, click the Color Styles drop-down menu, and choose Alpha. Set the Alpha Amount to 10%.

In the Timeline, click Keyframe 35 and set a Motion tween in the Property Inspector.

Move the Playhead to Keyframe 1, and press ⏎Enter to preview the animation.

You should see the text fade and zoom in and then fade and zoom out. If not, review the steps above.

With the animation of the word moments complete, now we just need to add a zoom-in segment for our final word: memories.

add timeline effects (cont.)

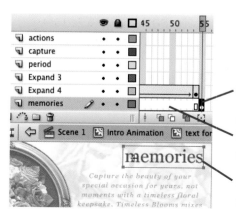

In the Timeline, select Frame 55 in the memories layer and insert a keyframe.

Move the Playhead to any of the frames before 55, and delete the memories text box—deleting it from Keyframe 1's entire span.

Click back in Keyframe 55 to select the memories text box.

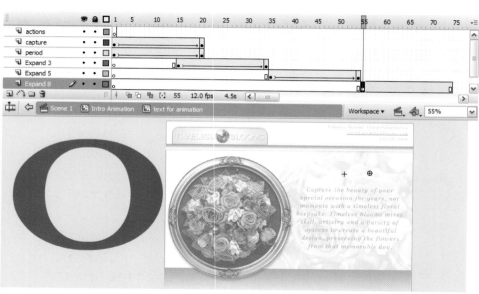

Add an Expand Timeline Effect with these settings:

Expand Style: Squeeze

Fragment Offset: 900

Fragment Size Height: 800 and Fragment Size Width: 600

That completes all of the text zoom-in and zoom-out animation. The only step remaining is to have memories fade in the same as moments does.

add animation to your web site

copy & paste motion

We want the zoom-in animation for memories to have the same alpha transparency tween as we created for moments. Rather than repeating the steps we took with moments, we can easily copy the animation parameters from moments and apply, or paste, them onto memories.

In the Timeline, click Keyframe 15 in the layer containing the zoom-in animation of moments.

Press and hold [Shift].

Click Keyframe 34 to select the range of frames.

Choose Edit > Timeline > Copy Motion, or right-click (Windows) or [Control]-click (Mac) on the selected frames, and choose Copy Motion from the drop-down menu.

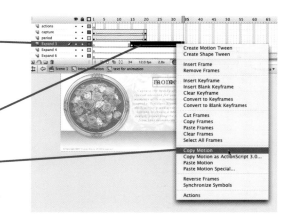

Click Keyframe 55 in the layer containing the zoom-in animation of memories to select the range of frames of the Expand Timeline Effect.

Choose Edit > Timeline > Paste Motion, or right-click (Windows) or [Control]-click (Mac) on the selected frames, and choose Paste Motion from the drop-down menu.

Press [←Enter] to preview the animation.

The animation looks great, but the word capture and the period disappear after Frame 20, and they need to stay visible while the other text zooms in and out.

We'll fix that next.

cut and paste frames

Remember that we want about a second to pass before any of the animations begin, but right now the capture and "." animation begins in Frame 1. We can cut the frames to the clipboard and paste them later in the Timeline.

Click Keyframe 1 in layer capture and drag down to the final keyframe in layer period to select the range of frames.

Right-click (Windows) or [Control]-click (Mac), and choose Cut Frames from the drop-down menu.

We want to paste the frames beginning at Frame 15, but first we need to remove the frames that are there.

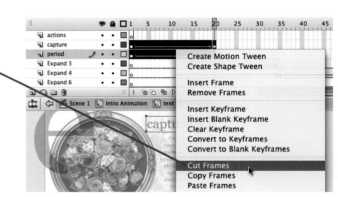

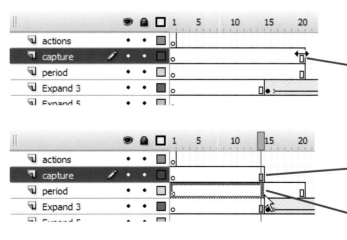

Click away from the selected frames to deselect them.

Move the cursor over the final keyframe in layer capture. Press [Ctrl] (Windows) or [⌘] (Mac). The cursor changes to a left/right arrow icon.

Click and drag to Frame 14. Release the cursor.

Repeat the steps in layer period.

add animation to your web site

Select Frame 15 in layer capture and drag down
to select the frame in layer period.

Right-click (Windows)
or ⌃Control-click (Mac) and
choose Paste Frames.

The text animation of the sliding text is now lined up with the first zooming text
animation, but it still disappears after its final keyframe.

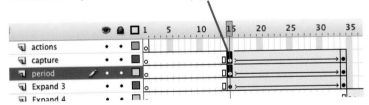

In layer capture, click Frame 74, the final frame of the
final zooming text animation, and insert a keyframe.

Repeat in layer period.

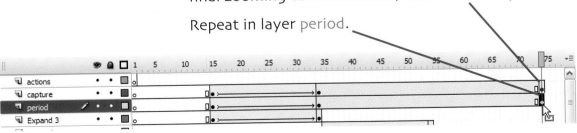

Press ↵Enter to preview the animation.

add animation to your web site

pause an animation

The animation looks great, but it all flies by too fast. We want to add a pause after moments zooms in and before it zooms back out, holding the word in place long enough for it to register with the viewer. (See extra bits on Page 74.)

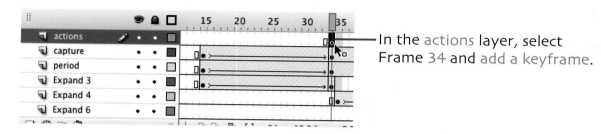

In the actions layer, select Frame 34 and add a keyframe.

Open the Actions panel and click to deselect the Script Assist button.

Enter this code in the Script pane:

```
stop();
pauseAnim = setInterval(this,"nextFrame",3000);
```

This code stops the animation, creates a timer, and moves to the next frame after 3 seconds (3000 milliseconds).

Select Keyframe 35 in the Timeline and add a keyframe.

Enter this code in the Script pane to delete the timer and play through the rest of the Timeline:

```
clearInterval(pauseAnim);
play();
```

add animation to your web site

preview your movie

Up to this point, we've previewed our animations in the Flash workspace. To preview the effect of the ActionScript pause, however, the animation has to be exported as a SWF file and viewed in the Flash Player.

We can do that quickly without going through the publishing process.

Choose Control > Test Movie, or press Ctrl ←Enter (Windows) or ⌘ ←Enter (Mac).

Flash quickly exports the SWF, opens a new Flash Player window, and plays the animation.

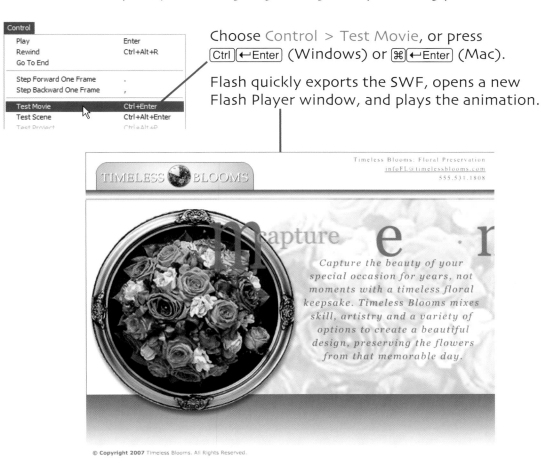

Notice the pause on the word moments; our ActionScript is working.

The animation loops because we haven't set any ActionScript in the final frame of the Timeline to stop it. We'll fix that later.

Click the Close button to close the Flash Player window.

add animation to your web site

add a transition effect

As the final piece in our intro animation, we want the contents animation
to appear about the same time that
moments zooms into place. We'll use a
Transition effect to fade them in.

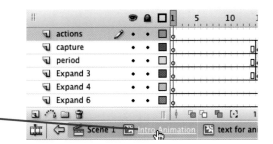

Return to symbol-editing mode on the
Intro Animation symbol.

Click Frame 1 to select the contents on the Stage, the image and boilerplate text
and text for animation symbols.

Right-click (Windows) or [Control]-
click (Mac) inside the bounding
box of the text and boilerplate
text instance and select Distribute
to Layers.

Click outside the bounding box of
the symbols to deselect them.

Click the bouquet image to select
the contents animation symbol.

Right-click (Windows) or [Control]-
click (Mac) the image. Choose
Timeline Effects > Transform/
Transition > Transition in the
drop-down menu.

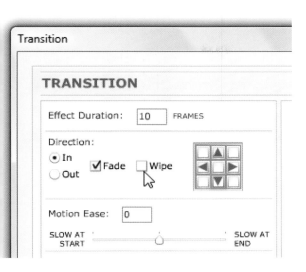

In the Transition dialog, enter a value of 10 frames for the Effect Duration.

Select In for Direction.

Select Fade.

Deselect Wipe.

Click OK.

Our original selection has been replaced with a new symbol. In the Property Inspector name the symbol instance contentAnimation.

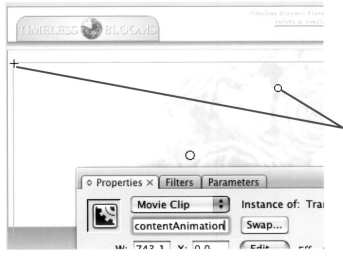

Note that because both objects on the Stage, the text for animation and contentAnimation symbols, have no visible contents in their first frames, neither is visible on the Stage.

They are both represented by and can be selected via the Registration Point markers.

Press Ctrl ←Enter (Windows) or ⌘ ←Enter (Mac) to preview the movie.

The fade-in looks good, but, as with the zooming text, it keeps repeating.

Next we'll use ActionScript to stop the two animations repeating and to have the fade-in of the contents animation occur about the time moments zooms into place.

add animation to your web site   **69**

control movie clips

First we'll stop the contents animation from repeating.

Click the Registration Point marker for symbol instance contentAnimation and choose Edit > Edit in place.

Read the warning dialog that appears, and click OK.

In the Timeline, insert a new layer. Name the layer actions.

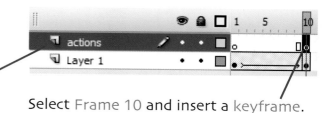

Select Frame 10 and insert a keyframe.

To stop the animation from repeating, enter stop(); in the Script pane.

We don't want this animation to play immediately when our site movie loads, so we'll put a Stop action in Frame 1 and use ActionScript elsewhere in the site movie to play it on cue.

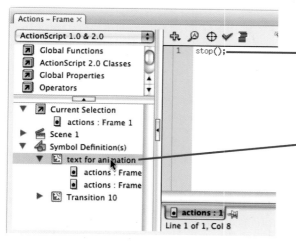

In the Timeline, click Frame 1 in the actions layer and enter stop(); in the Script pane.

That takes care of the ActionScript for the contents animation. Next we'll add ActionScript to the text animation.

In the Script Navigator, in the Actions panel, click to select Symbol Definition(s) > text for animation.

Symbol-editing mode is invoked on the text for animation symbol, and its Timeline is visible.

Our first task is to add ActionScript that will instruct the contents animation to play at the point we want.

Flash provides easy-to-use, pre-packaged actions called Behaviors. We'll use a Behavior to add the ActionScript we want.

add animation to your web site

add behaviors

In the actions layer, add a keyframe to Frame 30.

Open the Behaviors panel (Window > Behaviors).

Click the Add Behavior button and choose Movieclip > Goto and Play at Frame or Label in the drop-down menu.

In the Goto and Play at frame or label dialog, select _root > introAnimation > contentAnimation from the list.

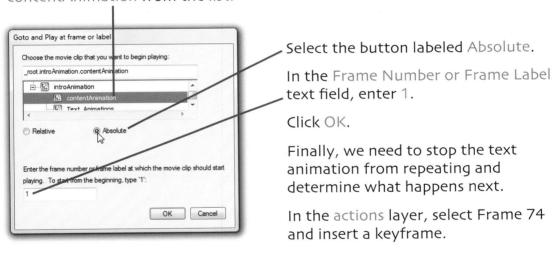

Select the button labeled Absolute.

In the Frame Number or Frame Label text field, enter 1.

Click OK.

Finally, we need to stop the text animation from repeating and determine what happens next.

In the actions layer, select Frame 74 and insert a keyframe.

In the Script pane, enter a Stop command, stop();.

Remember that our Intro Animation movie clip is playing in Keyframe intro of our main Timeline. Once the animations are complete, we want to move the main Timeline forward to Keyframe home, which will be visually identical but without the animation. Home is the Keyframe that users will navigate to and from as they move around the site. We do this so that viewers only see the animation when they first enter the site.

With Keyframe 74 still selected, click the Add Behavior button on the Behaviors panel.

In the drop-down, choose Movieclip > Goto and Stop at Frame or Label.

add animation to your web site

add behaviors (cont.)

In the Goto and Stop at frame or label dialog, select _root.

Select the button labeled Absolute.

In the Frame Number or Frame Label text field, enter home.

Click OK.

That's it. Our intro animation is complete. We only need to do one more step to make everything work the way we want.

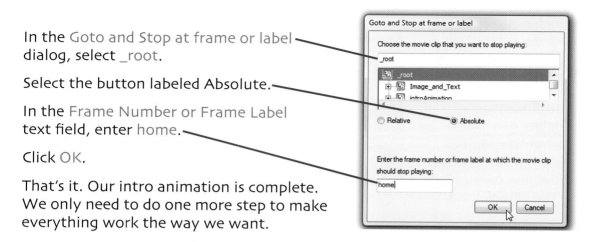

In the Edit Bar, select Scene 1 to return to our main Timeline. Select keyframe home in the actions layer.

Note that the text Capture Memories. is not visible. That's because the text for animations symbol is being used there, which would result in the text animation playing again when the action from our last step is executed and the Playhead moves to home.

Symbol types (Movie Clip, Button, Image) can be redefined on instances without changing the symbol's internal type. We'll do this to display the text we want.

Click the Registration Point marker for symbol text for animation.

In the Property Inspector, click the Instance Behaviors drop-down and choose Graphic.

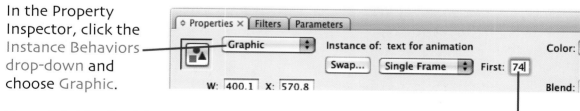

Enter 74 (the final frame of the text for animation symbol) in the First Frame text field.

The text appears just as we want.

Press Ctrl ←Enter (Windows) or ⌘ ←Enter (Mac) to preview your work in the Flash Player window.

add animation to your web site

extra bits

create a tween p. 52

- An animation is a series of static images (frames), where objects change incrementally from a beginning point to an end point. In Flash, we can define the beginning and end states with keyframes and let Flash generate the incremental frames. This method of creating the in-between frames is called tweening.

- There are two types of tweens in Flash: motion and shape. Motion tween is a bit of a misnomer, as it can be used to create changes not only in placement (motion) but also in alpha transparency, size, rotation, skew, and color effect. Motion tweens are applied to keyframes in a layer and only work when the layer contains only groups, symbol instances, and/or text blocks.

  Shape tweens work on shapes, not groups, symbols, or text blocks, and are used to change or "morph" the appearance of the shape.

- Ah, the Flash intro to a Web site—probably the most reviled Web phenomenon since the HTML Blink tag. The interminable wait to see the content you came to the site for in the first place and the frantic search for a Skip button, hoping the developer included one, made it all too much to bear and sent many viewers fleeing without ever getting into the site.

So what will we do? Create an intro, of course! However, we're going to create one that's done the right way—the evolved way. Here are the rules we'll follow to ensure that the animation doesn't irritate our viewers and doesn't get in the way of our content, which is, after all, the reason for having the site. The guidelines and how we're following them are as follows:

Make it simple and meaningful. Our animation will be elegant while actually furthering Timeless Blooms' marketing message of capturing the emotion of special events.

Don't let your intro obscure real content and navigation. Allow users to "get on with it" without waiting for the intro to finish. Our content and navigation buttons will be available from Frame 1.

Once viewers have seen the animation, don't make them view it again when navigating back to the home page from other areas of the site. This is why we created two keyframes in our main Timeline, one for the intro and one for home.

extra bits

pause an animation p. 66

- You've already seen that you can add time between animations by adding blank frames. We could add frames between the animation segments here, but we want a 3-second pause, which would require adding 36 blank frames, and our Timeline is already long and unwieldy. Instead, we'll use ActionScript to pause the Timeline.

- As a beginning Flash developer without deep understanding of ActionScript or other programming languages, you can often find code examples to use without understanding the technicalities of what they do.

  There are many resources on the Web that provide such examples. Visit the Adobe Developer Forums at www.adobe.com/support/forums/.

  Also, you can type a question like "how to pause a movie in Flash" in a Web search engine like Google and get pointers to multiple developer sites offering code help.

- The code we use in this step is very simple. You can copy and paste it into any of your projects to create a pause in animation. To change the amount of time, simply change the number. Time is in milliseconds (1000ths) so 3000 equals 3 seconds.

7. build a navigation system

So far, we've created a great-looking home page with an engaging introductory animation. But the site doesn't have any real content yet. It's like a movie with opening credits but no scenes revealing the plot.

In this chapter, we add keyframes to the main Timeline to define the site's sections, and create interactive buttons to navigate between those sections.

add sections to the site

Before we create buttons for navigating the site, we need to have some places to navigate to. We need to add the other sections of our site to the Timeline.

The Web site has four sections: Home, Info, Gallery, and Pricing.

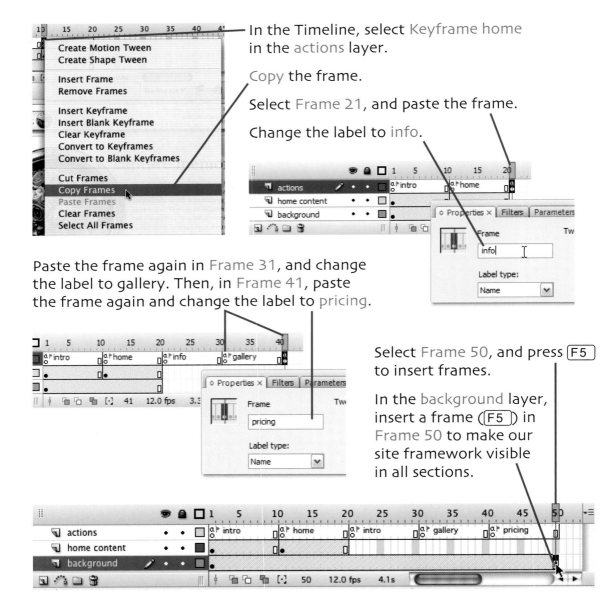

In the Timeline, select Keyframe home in the actions layer.

Copy the frame.

Select Frame 21, and paste the frame.

Change the label to info.

Paste the frame again in Frame 31, and change the label to gallery. Then, in Frame 41, paste the frame again and change the label to pricing.

Select Frame 50, and press [F5] to insert frames.

In the background layer, insert a frame ([F5]) in Frame 50 to make our site framework visible in all sections.

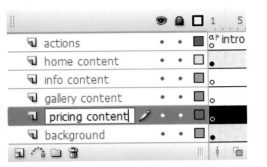

Add three new layers, one for each of the sections we've just created. Name them info content, gallery content, and pricing content.

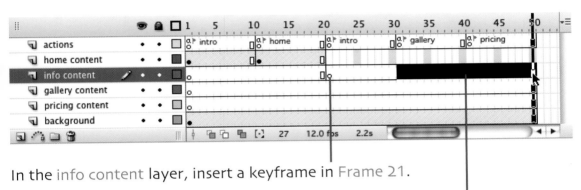

In the info content layer, insert a keyframe in Frame 21.

Click Frame 31 and drag to Frame 50, selecting the span of frames.

Delete the frames ([Shift][F5]).

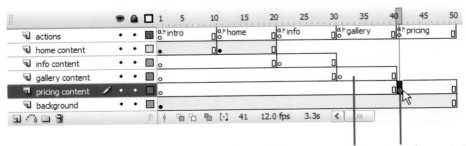

Repeat the steps in the gallery content layer, adding a keyframe at Frame 31 and deleting Frames 41 through 50.

In the pricing content layer, insert a keyframe in Frame 41.

build a navigation system

create buttons

With our sections defined, we need to create a button for each of the sections. Button symbols provide an easy method for creating the type of interactive, multistate button we're accustomed to seeing on the Web. The first step will be to create a button master that will serve as an easily edited template for all of the buttons. (See extra bits on Page 94.)

The background appearance of the buttons will be a variation of the linear gradient we used in the site framework. We'll use a copy of the rectangle as a starting point for the button background.

In the Library panel, double-click to open the Framework Parts folder. Double-click the symbol icon for the symbol Framework to invoke symbol-editing mode.

Select the rectangle with the linear gradient fill near the top of the Stage.

Copy the rectangle to the clipboard.

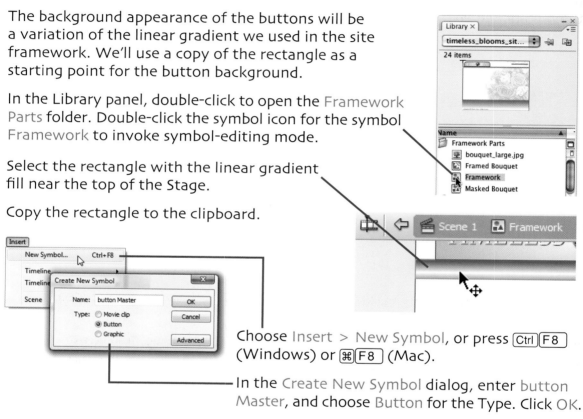

Choose Insert > New Symbol, or press Ctrl F8 (Windows) or ⌘ F8 (Mac).

In the Create New Symbol dialog, enter button Master, and choose Button for the Type. Click OK.

Flash creates the new symbol and opens it for editing. Note the special button Timeline with a specially labeled frame for each button state.

Rename Layer 1 button bkgd.

Paste the rectangle on the Stage.

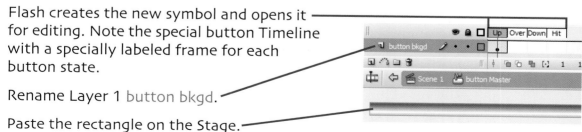

1 In the Property Inspector, change the width to 60.

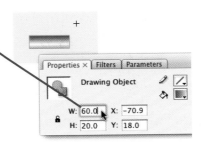

Centering the button parts on the registration point of the button symbol will help make arranging objects easier. We'll center the rectangle now.

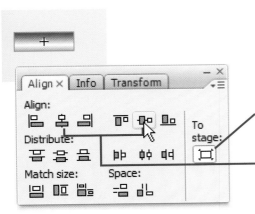

2 With the rectangle still selected, open the Align panel.

3 Click the Align To Stage button to align the rectangle to the symbol's registration point.

4 Click the Align Horizontal Center button and then the Align Vertical Center button to center the rectangle on the registration point.

We'll be working on the button appearance for a while, so it's a good idea to zoom in with the Zoom tool.

The appearance of the button background in the Over state will be different than that in the Up state. It will still be a variation on the gradient so let's get the rectangle placed in the Over state before we begin changing it.

5 Click the Over frame and insert a keyframe, which places a copy of the rectangle in the frame.

create buttons (cont.)

Click back in the Up keyframe, auto-matically selecting the rectangle.

In the Color panel, double-click the pointer on the left end of the gradient definition bar to open the swatches pop-up. Choose our light purple color.

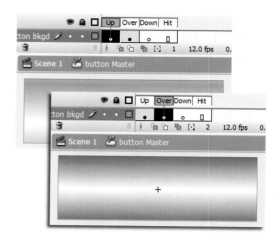

Now we have a different background appearance between the Up and Over states. That's enough for the background for now.

Next we'll add some placeholder text to our button master. Keeping in mind that the text will be changed for each button that is made from this master and knowing that the text will be placed in multiple frames (and even different Timelines later in this chapter), we want to be smart about how we create the text so that changing it will be very easy.

To accomplish this, we'll create a symbol of the text and place instances of that symbol in the places we need it. We'll then be able to change the text only once, but have it update throughout the different frames and Timelines.

Add a new layer and name it button text.

Choose the Text tool, and set the following attributes in the Property Inspector.

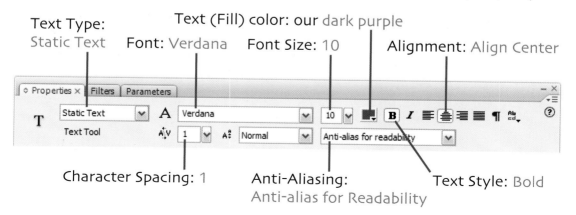

Text Type: Static Text

Text (Fill) color: our dark purple

Font: Verdana

Font Size: 10

Alignment: Align Center

Character Spacing: 1

Anti-Aliasing: Anti-alias for Readability

Text Style: Bold

build a navigation system

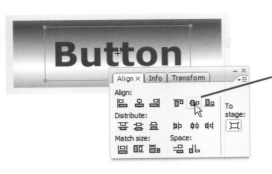

Click the Stage and type Button.

Choose the Selection tool to set the text.

Use the Align panel to center the text box on the registration point.

Convert the text box to a symbol (F8).

In the Convert to Symbol dialog enter button Master text, choose Graphic, and click the center Registration point to help center the text in the button. Click OK.

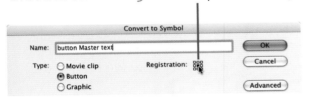

The Down state is displayed when a user clicks the button. For now we'll define it to be the same as the Over state.

Click the Down frame in the button text layer and drag down to select the frame in the button bkgd layer.

Insert a frame (F5).

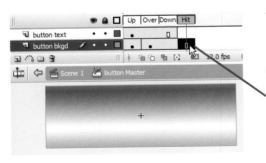

The Hit state defines the area of the button that responds to mouse activity. For our button, that area is the same as the background.

Select frame Hit in the button bkgd layer and insert a frame (F5).

We now have the basics of a working button.

preview button actions

We can preview our button actions inside Flash. Let's place an instance on the Stage and see how our button works so far.

Click Scene 1 in the Edit Bar to exit symbol-editing mode.

Add a new layer to the Timeline, and name it buttons. Drag the layer to position it between the home content and actions layers.

In the Library panel, click the button Master symbol, and drag it onto the Stage over the linear gradient rectangle and near the right edge of the Stage.

With the Selection tool, position the button instance vertically over the linear gradient rectangle.

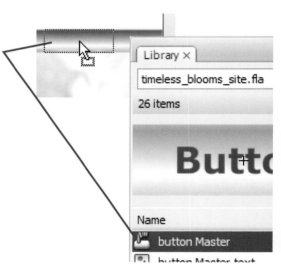

Choose Control > Enable Simple Buttons.

Move the cursor over the button to view the Over state.

Click to view the Down state; right now it's the same as the Over state so you won't see any change.

Our button works great, but it's kind of boring. Let's work on punching it up.

Choose Control > Enable Simple Buttons again to turn off button preview.

animate a button state

To make our button more interesting, we're going to add a short animation to the Over state and add a slight offset to the Down state.

With the Selection tool, double-click the button instance to edit it.

In the Timeline, click the Down frame of the button bkgd layer and insert a keyframe so the animation we create for the Over state won't also be in the Down state.

Click the Over frame of the button bkgd layer, selecting the gradient-filled rectangle.

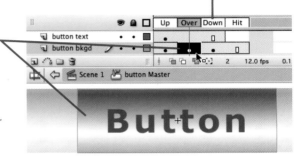

Convert the selection to a symbol ((F8)). Name the symbol button Master bkgd over, choose Movie Clip and center Registration.

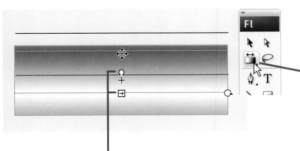

Double-click the new symbol to edit it.

Insert a keyframe in Frame 6.

Select the Gradient Transform tool and click to select the rectangle.

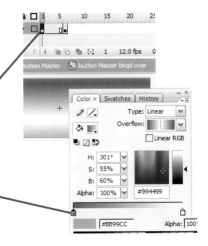

Click and drag the center point handle up a bit to raise the halfway point of the transition, moving the white area nearer to the center of the rectangle.

Choose the Selection tool.

Select Frame 1 in the Timeline, automatically selecting the rectangle.

In the Color panel, double-click the pointer on the left end of the gradient definition bar to open the swatches pop-up. Choose our light purple color.

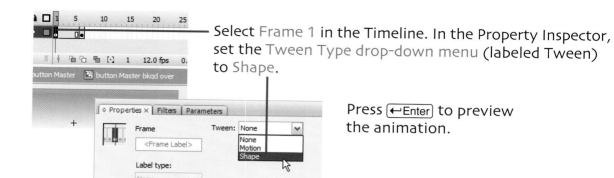

Select Frame 1 in the Timeline. In the Property Inspector, set the Tween Type drop-down menu (labeled Tween) to Shape.

Press (←Enter) to preview the animation.

We need to add a Stop action, or the animation will loop repeatedly when the user's mouse is over the button.

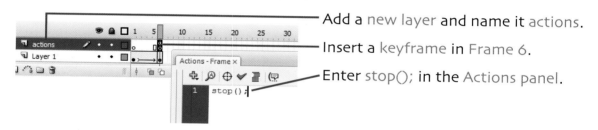

Add a new layer and name it actions.

Insert a keyframe in Frame 6.

Enter stop(); in the Actions panel.

Now we'll make a small animation of the text to make it more readable over the darker gradient that appears at the end of the background animation.

Click button Master in the Edit Bar to exit symbol-editing mode for the movie clip.

Select the Over frame in the button text layer. Insert a keyframe.

Select the Down frame in the button text layer and insert a keyframe.

Click back on the Over frame, automatically selecting the text symbol instance.

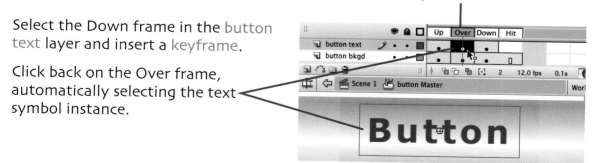

Convert the selection to a symbol ([F8]).

Name the symbol button Master text over, choose Movie Clip for the Type, and choose center Registration.

Double-click the new symbol to edit it.

Insert a keyframe in Frame 6.

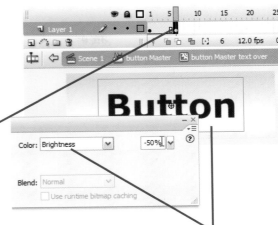

With the symbol instance selected in Frame 6, click the Color Styles drop-down menu in the Property Inspector and select Brightness. Set the brightness value to -50% to give the text a very dark purple color.

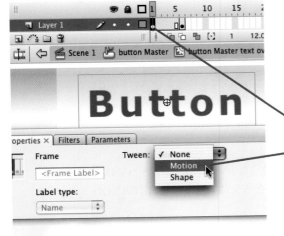

Click to select Frame 1.

In the Property Inspector, set the Tween Type drop-down menu to Motion.

We need to add a Stop action for this animation.

Add a new layer and name it actions.

Insert a keyframe in Frame 6.

Enter stop(); in the Actions panel.

animate a button (cont.)

Finally, for our Down state we want to move the text down and to the right one pixel.

Click button Master in the Edit Bar to exit symbol-editing mode for the movie clip.

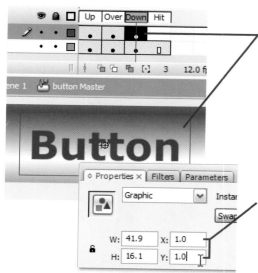

Move the Playhead to the Down frame, and click the text symbol instance to select it.

In the Property Inspector, add 1 to the x and y values of the selection. If your text symbol is still properly aligned with the registration point, the values should both be 0.0. Change each value to 1.0.

We're done editing the button, so exit symbol-editing mode by clicking Scene 1 in the Edit Bar.

The Enable Simple Buttons feature won't show us the animated Over state, so we'll have to preview our buttons in the Flash Player.

Choose Control > Test Movie, or press [Control][⏎Enter] (Windows) or [⌘][⏎Enter] (Mac).

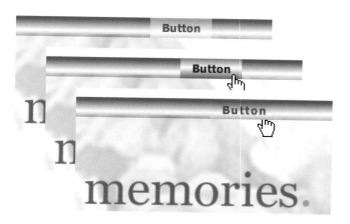

Move the cursor over the button to see the Over state animation, then click to see the text offset for the Down state.

Close the Flash Player window.

build a navigation system

add button sound

As the final touch to our button, we're going to add a click sound to the Down state.

Choose File > Import > Import to Library. In the Import to Library dialog, navigate to the development_files folder. Select the file btn_click.wav, and click Open.

Double-click the button Master instance to edit it.

Add a new layer, and name it sound.

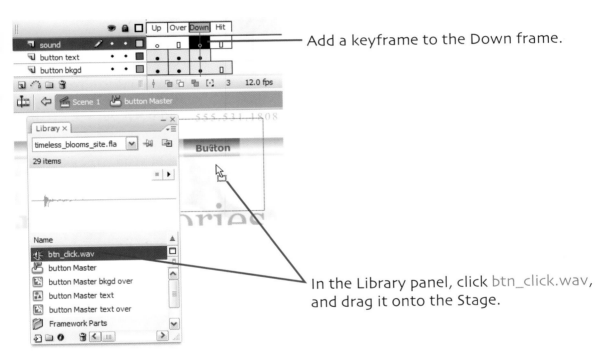

Add a keyframe to the Down frame.

In the Library panel, click btn_click.wav, and drag it onto the Stage.

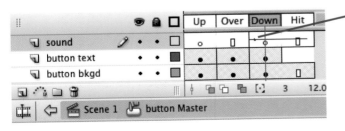

Notice the marker in the Timeline, signifying a sound object in the frame.

Exit symbol-editing mode.

If you want to test the sound, turn on Enable Simple Buttons and click the button.

duplicate buttons

Now that we've completed our button design, we need to make copies for each of the sections of our site.

We'll make duplicates of the different symbols that make up a button and then use symbol swapping to change out one symbol for another. This can be a difficult series of steps, but by using consistent naming conventions for symbols and dividing the steps into three smaller groups, we can do it successfully.

A In the first group of steps we make duplicates of the Master symbols:

1 In the Library panel, right-click (Windows) or (Control)-click (Mac) the button Master symbol, and choose Duplicate from the drop-down menu.

2 In the Duplicate Symbol dialog, name the symbol button Home, and click OK.

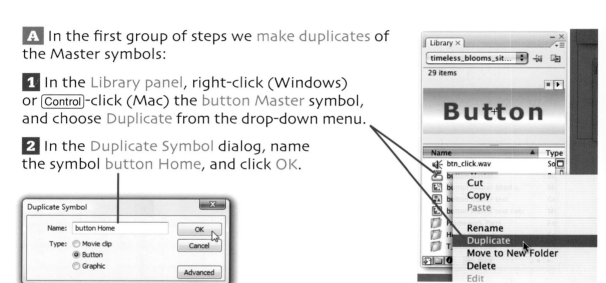

3 Now right-click (Windows) or (Control)-click (Mac) the button Master text symbol in the Library panel, and choose Duplicate from the drop-down menu.

4 In the Duplicate Symbol dialog, name the symbol button Home text, and click OK.

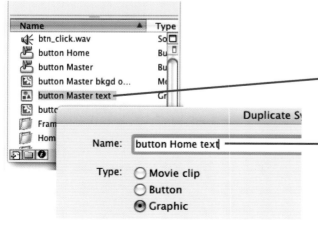

build a navigation system

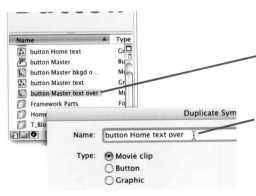

5 Now right-click (Windows) or (Control)-click (Mac) the button Master text over symbol in the Library panel, and choose Duplicate from the drop-down menu.

6 In the Duplicate Symbol dialog, name the symbol button Home text over, and click OK.

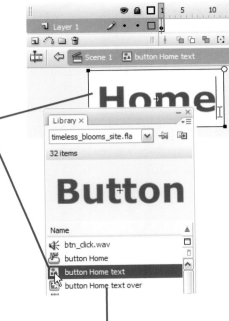

B Next we change the text in the text symbol to match the section.

In the Library panel, double-click the button Home text symbol icon to edit it. Change the text to Home.

C In the final series of steps, we'll swap the instances of the Master Symbols with the symbols we've created for that section.

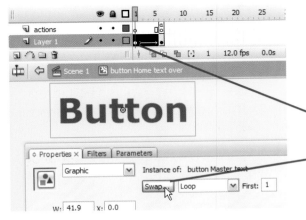

1 In the Library panel, double-click the button Home text over symbol icon to edit it.

2 In Keyframe 1, select the button Master text symbol instance.

3 Click the Swap Symbol button in the Property Inspector.

duplicate buttons (cont.)

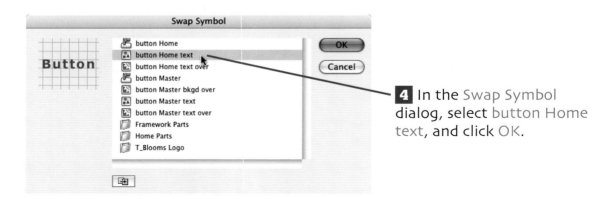

4 In the Swap Symbol dialog, select button Home text, and click OK.

5 Move the Playhead to Keyframe 6 and swap the symbol there. Note that the Brightness Color Style remains applied.

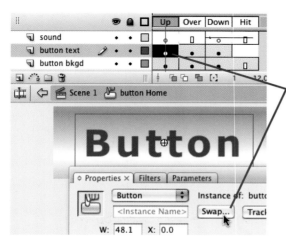

6 Now double-click the button Home symbol icon in the Library panel.

7 In the Up keyframe, select the button Master text symbol and click the Swap Symbol button in the Property Inspector.

build a navigation system

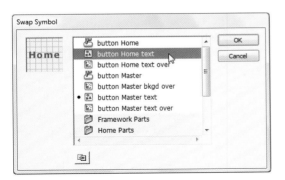

8 In the Swap Symbol dialog, select button Home text, and click OK.

9 Repeat the steps to swap the symbol in the Down keyframe.

10 Click Keyframe Over and select the button Master text over symbol instance.

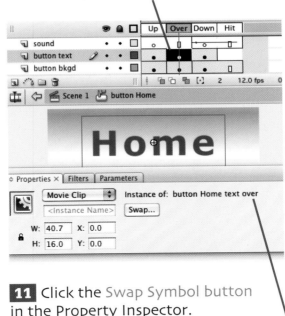

11 Click the Swap Symbol button in the Property Inspector.

12 In the Swap Symbol dialog, select button Home text over, and click OK.

Exit symbol-editing mode.

Repeat the duplication process, making button symbols for Info, Gallery, and Pricing.

build a navigation system

layout buttons

With a button for each of our sections complete, we can add them to the layout.

First delete the button Master instance from the Stage.

In the layers column of the Timeline, select the buttons layer to make it the current layer.

From the Library panel, drag out an instance of each of the buttons into the buttons layer, ordering them as shown here. (Don't worry about spacing or alignment; we'll fix that in a minute.)

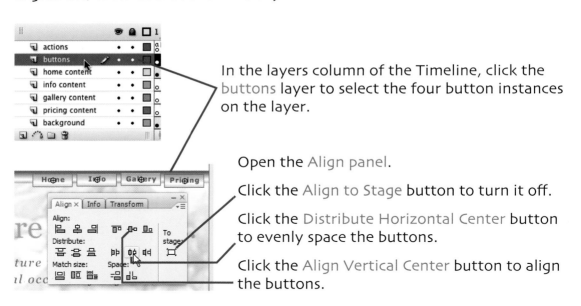

In the layers column of the Timeline, click the buttons layer to select the four button instances on the layer.

Open the Align panel.

Click the Align to Stage button to turn it off.

Click the Distribute Horizontal Center button to evenly space the buttons.

Click the Align Vertical Center button to align the buttons.

Zoom in to enlarge your view of the buttons.

With the Selection tool, drag to position the buttons accurately on top of the gradient-filled rectangle. If needed, use the arrow keys to nudge them into place.

Choose Control > Test Movie, or press Ctrl ←Enter (Windows) or ⌘ ←Enter (Mac) to preview the movie in the Flash Player. Test out the buttons to see how they operate.

build a navigation system

add actionscript

With our site sections defined and the buttons created to navigate to them, let's hook the two up. We'll use Behaviors to easily establish functional navigation.

Select the Home button.

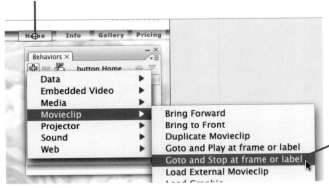

Open the Behaviors panel. Click the Add Behavior button. In the drop-down menu, choose Movieclip > Goto and Stop at frame or label.

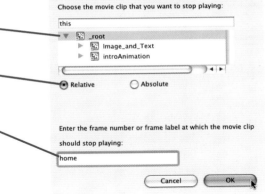

In the Goto and Stop at frame or label dialog, select _root in the list.

Confirm that the radio button labeled Relative is selected.

In the Frame Number or Frame Label text field, enter home.

Click OK.

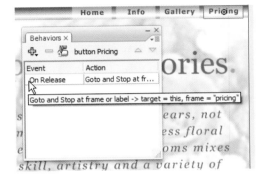

The Behavior is now listed in the panel and can be edited later, if necessary.

Select the Info button. Repeat the steps to add the Goto and Stop at Frame or Label behavior. Enter info in the Frame Number or Frame Label text field.

Repeat the process for the other two buttons, pointing each to its corresponding labeled keyframe.

extra bits

create buttons p. 78

- Buttons have different images (referred to as states) that display based upon user action. The Up state displays by default; the Over state displays when the user moves the mouse over the button; and the Down state displays when the button is clicked. A fourth state, Hit, is never displayed but is used to define the active area of the button.

- In most cases, you'll use the same graphic elements for all of your buttons. When you're working out the design, work with the text of the longest name you'll need. This ensures that the graphic fits all of your buttons and you won't have to make frustrating fixes later. In our project, the button was originally sized to the word Gallery button because it is just a little bit wider than Pricing.

8. add inside sections of the web site

In this chapter we begin filling in content in the different sections of the site. We'll use both basic and complex techniques to present each different type of content in the most effective way. In this chapter we'll:

Style text with Cascading Style Sheets.

Create input text fields for user interaction.

Load HTML-formatted text on the fly.

Set text dynamically.

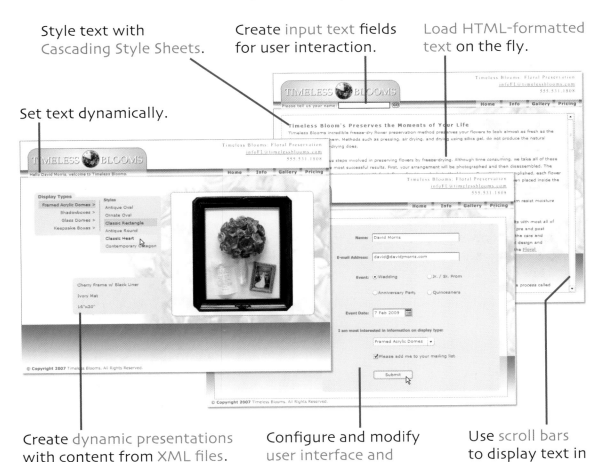

Create dynamic presentations with content from XML files.

Configure and modify user interface and forms components.

Use scroll bars to display text in limited space.

95

import symbols

The benefits of symbols as reusable and easy-to-update objects are not limited to their use in a single document. You can import symbols from other files and maintain a link to the original source, allowing quick updates to objects in multiple files. On a large site with multiple Flash files or if you have symbols that you use time and again, importing symbols from a single source can be a great time-saver.

You can open a file's library without opening the complete Flash file.

In the Panels Dock, click the double arrow to expand the panel view. Open the Library panel if it's not already open.

Select File > Import > Open External Library.

In the Open as Library dialog, navigate to the development_files folder. Select the file Libraries for Ch 08 and Ch 09.fla, and click Open.

A new Library panel with the file's symbols is opened.

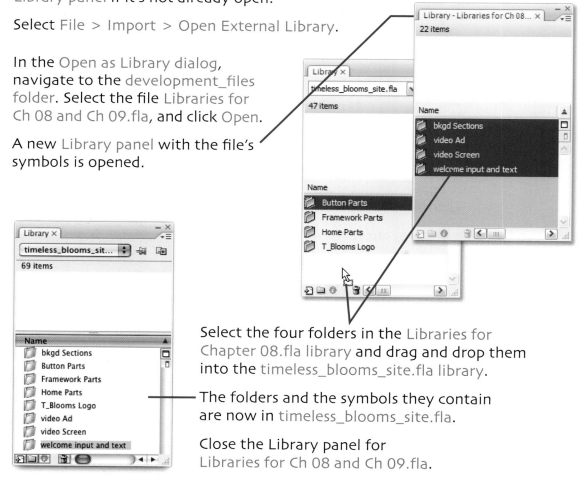

Select the four folders in the Libraries for Chapter 08.fla library and drag and drop them into the timeless_blooms_site.fla library.

The folders and the symbols they contain are now in timeless_blooms_site.fla.

Close the Library panel for Libraries for Ch 08 and Ch 09.fla.

add inside sections of the web site

update symbols

To update a symbol shared between files, we make changes to the symbol in the original source file and then pull the updates into the other files with instances of the symbol.

Let's make an update to one of the symbols we just imported.

Open the file Libraries for Ch 08 and Ch 09.fla.

In the Library panel, open the folder welcome input and text.

Double-click the symbol icon for button GO to invoke symbol-editing mode on the button.

With the Selection tool, click to select the GO text box.

In the Property Inspector, click the Fill color well, and choose our dark purple.

Save the file (File > Save) and close it.

Back in the timeless_blooms_site.fla file, open the welcome input and text folder and select the symbol button GO.

In the Preview pane, note that the text is still black.

Right-click (Windows) or [Control]-click (Mac) the symbol and choose Properties from the drop-down menu.

update symbols (cont.)

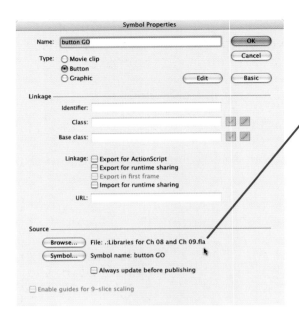

In the Symbol Properties dialog, click Advanced to expand the dialog.

In the Source area, note that Libraries for Ch 08 and Ch 09.fla is shown as the source.

Click OK to close the dialog.

Right-click (Windows) or Control-click (Mac) the symbol button GO again and choose Update from the drop-down menu.

In the Update Library Items dialog, note that it shows that 1 item needs to be updated.

With button GO checked in the Label column, choose Update.

Note that the dialog shows 1 item updated.

Choose Close to dismiss the dialog.

In the Library panel, select the symbol button GO.

In the Preview pane, note the updated appearance.

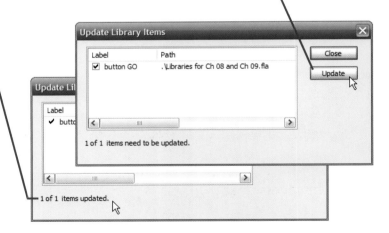

The button GO symbol and the other symbols you've imported are used throughout this chapter and the next to allow you to execute new, advanced tasks rather than spending time, and pages, repeating tasks you've already learned.

create input text

Text boxes in Flash are one of three types: static, dynamic, or input. So far, we've only worked with static text. We'll work with dynamic text later in this chapter; now we're going to create input text, meaning a text box for user input.

For our site, we'll add an input text field for users to enter their name. Then we'll add their name dynamically to some text, personalizing their experience.

In the Timeline, add a new layer above the layer buttons and name it welcome.

In the Library, navigate to welcome input and text > bkgd Welcome and drag an instance onto the gradient-filled rectangle, below the logo.

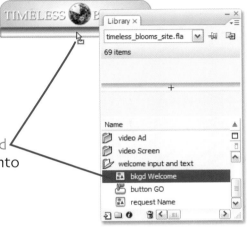

Convert the selection to a symbol (F8). Name the symbol msg Welcome, then choose Movie Clip and center Registration.

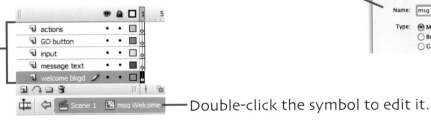

Double-click the symbol to edit it.

Insert four new layers in the Timeline. Name the layers as shown.

Select the layer message text and drag an instance of welcome input and text > request Name onto the Stage, placing it over the background rectangle near the left edge.

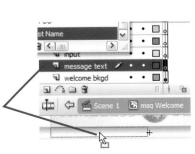

create input text (cont.)

Select layer Go button and drag an instance of welcome input and text > button Go onto the Stage, placing it near the right edge of the background rectangle.

Select layer input.

Choose the Text tool and set these properties in the Property Inspector:

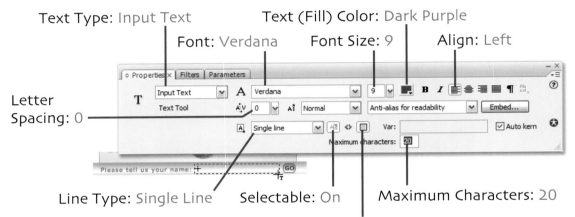

Text Type: Input Text
Text (Fill) Color: Dark Purple
Font: Verdana
Font Size: 9
Align: Left
Letter Spacing: 0
Line Type: Single Line
Selectable: On
Show Border Around Text: On
Maximum Characters: 20

Click and drag out a text box from the right of name: to near the button GO symbol instance.

In the Property Inspector, enter name for the Variable.

A variable represents a value that can be set or modified by an action. Here, the name that the user enters in the input field, let's say David, will be the value of a variable called name.

Choose the Selection tool to set the input text box. Use the Selection tool or arrow keys to adjust the placement of the text box.

Test the movie. Click in the input field and enter your name to see that it does allow user input. Pressing Enter or clicking the GO button doesn't do anything yet, but we'll set that up next.

Close the Flash Player window.

add inside sections of the web site

set text dynamically

With our input text field created, we'll now create a dynamic text block that will insert the user's name into a message, providing a personalized experience.

First we need to set up an Action defining what will happen when the user enters their name.

Still in editing mode on the msg Welcome symbol, insert a keyframe in Frame 10 of all layers but the welcome bkgd layer.

Insert a frame in Frame 19 of all the layers.

In the actions layer, label Frame 1 request and Frame 10 message.

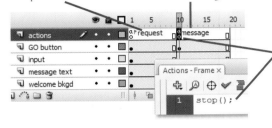

In the Actions panel, add a stop command (stop();) in keyframes request and message.

In the keyframe message, delete the request Name symbol instance, the input text box, and the button GO symbol.

Move the Playhead to keyframe request.

Select the button GO symbol.

Open the Actions panel.

Click the Script Assist button to turn it on.

In the Actions Toolbox, click Global Functions to open the functions list.

Click to open the Movie Clip Control functions list.

Double-click the on function. This function responds to specified events in the Flash movie or from user input.

add inside sections of the web site

set text dynamically (cont.)

In the Toolbar, select Release.

Select Key Press and press the Enter key on the keyboard to set < Enter > as the key press event to respond to.

With the first line of code still selected in the Script pane, click Global Functions > Timeline Control in the Actions Toolbox.

Double-click goto.

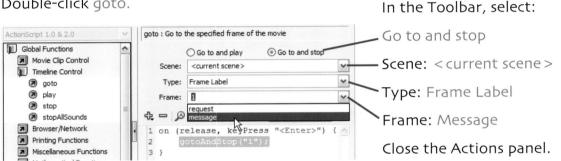

In the Toolbar, select:

Go to and stop

Scene: < current scene >

Type: Frame Label

Frame: Message

Close the Actions panel.

Test the movie. Enter a name in the input text field and press Enter or click the GO button. The name request text, input text box, and GO button disappear as the symbol's Timeline moves to the message keyframe, which doesn't yet have any content.

Close the Flash Player window.

Select keyframe message in layer message text.

Choose the Text tool.

In the Property Inspector change the Text Type to Dynamic Text and Line Type to Single Line.

Set Selectable and Show Border Around Text to off.

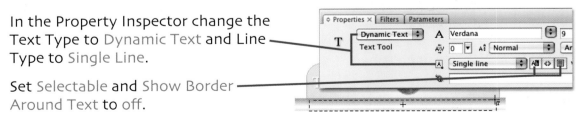

Click and drag out a text box from the left side of the background rectangle to the right edge.

add inside sections of the web site

In the Property Inspector enter msgWelcome in the Variable field.

Choose the Selection tool to set the input text box.

Use the selection key or arrow keys to adjust the placement of the text box.

You've now set up a text box and assigned a variable named msgWelcome as the contents of that box. Once an action occurs that gives the variable msgWelcome a value, that value will become the text inside the box.

Select keyframe message in the layer actions.

In the Actions panel, click Script Assist to turn it off.

Place the cursor after the stop action code and press [Enter] twice.

Enter this code:

msgWelcome = "Hello " + name + ", welcome to Timeless Blooms.";

That's it; you've just assigned a value to the variable msgWelcome. The value puts together (concatenates in programming speak) the text between the first set of quotes, the value of the variable name from our input text box, and the text between the second set of quotes.

Click Scene 1 in the Edit Bar to exit symbol-editing mode.

Test the movie.

Enter a name in the input text field and press [Enter] or click the GO button.

Now you have a personalized message on your site greeting each visitor.

add inside sections of the web site   **103**

create scrolling text

Content for the Info section is contained in an HTML file that loads dynamically when our site movie is played. There's more text for the section than will fit within the content area of our layout, so to fit the text into the area we'll create a text box with an attached scroll bar component.

In the main file Timeline, select keyframe info in layer info content.

From the Library panel, drag out an instance of bkgd Sections > bkgd Content.

In the Property Inspector, set the position values to x = 20 and y = 110.

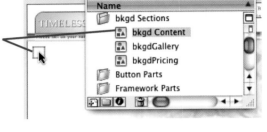

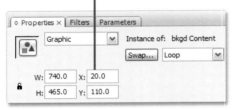

Choose the Text tool and set the following values in the Property Inspector:

Line Type: Text Type: Font: Font   Text (Fill) Color:
Multiline   Dynamic Text   Verdana   Size: 9   Dark Purple

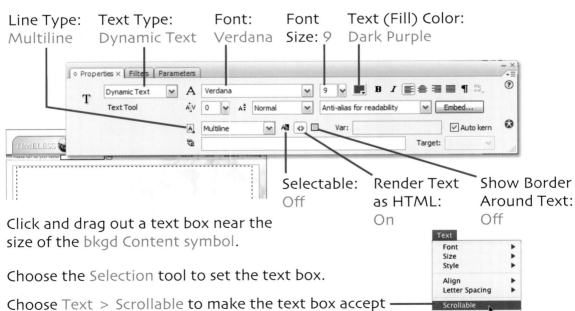

Selectable: Render Text   Show Border
Off   as HTML: Around Text:
                On   Off

Click and drag out a text box near the size of the bkgd Content symbol.

Choose the Selection tool to set the text box.

Choose Text > Scrollable to make the text box accept more text than will fit within its dimensions.

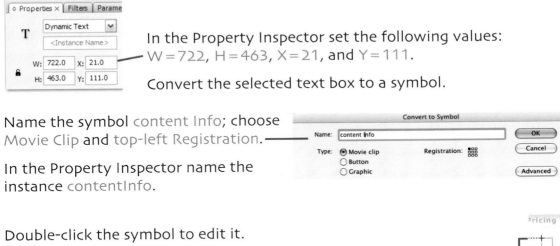

In the Property Inspector set the following values: W = 722, H = 463, X = 21, and Y = 111.

Convert the selected text box to a symbol.

Name the symbol content Info; choose Movie Clip and top-left Registration.

In the Property Inspector name the instance contentInfo.

Double-click the symbol to edit it.

Select the text box and give it an instance name of textInfo.

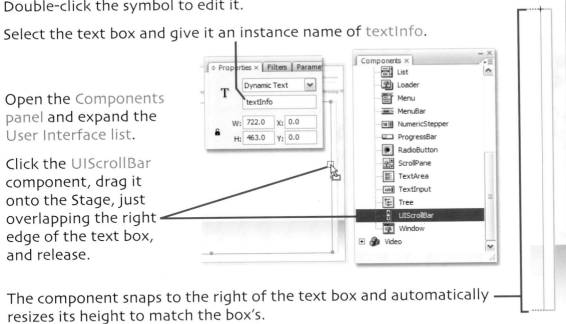

Open the Components panel and expand the User Interface list.

Click the UIScrollBar component, drag it onto the Stage, just overlapping the right edge of the text box, and release.

The component snaps to the right of the text box and automatically resizes its height to match the box's.

Click Scene 1 in the Edit Bar to exit symbol-editing mode.

With a scrolling text box created to contain it, we're ready to set up loading the HTML file containing the content for the Info section.

add inside sections of the web site

load html text

The text-editing capabilities in Flash are best suited for small amounts like we've worked with so far. But for larger chunks of text it's often more efficient to keep the text in an external format that is loaded into the movie at runtime (when the movie plays in Flash Player). Placing text with simple HTML formatting in text (TXT) files makes updating the content much faster and easier—you can update the text file independent of your Flash movie.

We'll place the function (set of instructions) for loading a text file in the first frame of our main Timeline.

Select keyframe intro in the actions layer.

In the Actions panel enter the code as shown. Commented text, preceded by //, is not required; it provides some basic explanation of what the code does.

```
1   stop();
2   // create a variable for a LoadVars function and name the variable myLoadVars
3   var myLoadVars:LoadVars = new LoadVars();
4   // when myLoadVars is called from Frame 1 of symbol content Info execute this function
5   myLoadVars.onLoad = function (success) {
6       // if the external text file was loaded into memory successfully load the text into
7       // the dynamic text box textInfo
8       if (success) {
9           _root.contentInfo.textInfo.htmlText = myLoadVars.textInfo;
10      // if the text file did not load successfully display an error message in textInfo
11      } else {
12          _root.contentInfo.textInfo.text = "An error occurred loading the requested content.";
13      }
14  }
```

Actions - Frame ×

Script Assist

actions : 1

Line 14 of 14, Col 2

You can use this code in your own projects, just remember to change any reference to "textInfo" to match the instance name you give your target text box.

OK, we've told Flash how to load the text file. Now we need to tell it when and where.

In the Library panel, double-click the icon for symbol content Info to invoke symbol-editing mode.

add inside sections of the web site

Insert a new layer and name it actions.

Select Keyframe 1 in the actions layer.

In the Actions panel enter this code:

_root.myLoadVars.load("textInfo.txt");

Exit symbol-editing mode.

Save the file, and minimize the Flash application to view your desktop.

Locate your development_files folder. Inside the folder, locate the file textInfo.txt. This is the text file containing our Info section content. We need to open it and add some text that identifies it for Flash. Double-click to open the file. The file will open in Notepad (Windows) or TextEdit (Mac).

You'll note that the text file is not formatted in a standard way with carriage returns; this is a requirement for Flash to display the text correctly.

Click to place the insertion point at the beginning of the file, before the text < textformat.

Enter textInfo =. Save and close the file.

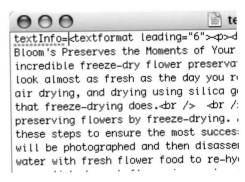

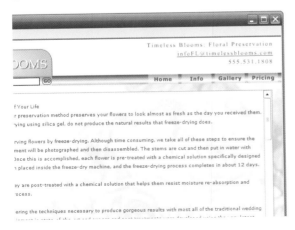

Make the Flash application visible again and test the movie, [Ctrl][←Enter] (Windows) or [⌘][←Enter] (Mac).

Click the Info button, and you'll see that the text box has been populated with the contents of the text file—it's not pretty, but it's there.

Next we'll load a Cascading Style Sheet (CSS) to apply formatting to the text.

style text with css

Cascading Style Sheets (CSS), used to define consistent appearances across sites, can be loaded into Flash to format text.

In the Library panel, double-click the icon for symbol content Info to invoke symbol-editing mode.

Select Keyframe 1 in the actions layer and enter the code as shown. Note that the existing code in the Actions panel (_root.myLoadVars.load("textInfo.txt");) is embedded in the new code in line 14. You can cut and paste it into place.

```
1   // create a variable for a StyleSheet object and name it cssStyles
2   var cssStyles:TextField.StyleSheet = new TextField.StyleSheet();
3   // load the external style sheet into memory
4   cssStyles.load("stylesSite.css");
5   // after attempting to load the style sheet, execute the
6   // function and pass on whether loading was a success or not
7   cssStyles.onLoad = function (success) {
8       // if informed that the style sheet loaded successfully apply the
9       // style sheet to the dynamic text box textInfo and then load the
10      // external text file into memory and notify the myLoadVars function
11      // in keyframe intro if loading the text file was successful or not
12      if (success) {
13          textInfo.styleSheet = cssStyles;
14          _root.myLoadVars.load("textInfo.txt");
15      // if the style sheet did not load successfully
16      // display an error message in textInfo
17      } else {
18          textInfo.text = "An error occurred loading the requested content.";
19      }
20  }
```

Test the movie, Ctrl ←Enter (Windows) or ⌘ ←Enter (Mac).

Click the Info button, and you'll see that not only is the text box populated with the contents of the text file, but that the text is formatted nicely.

Our Info section is now complete!

Close the Flash Player and save your Flash file.

load xml content

In order to decrease the initial download time when a user visits a site, we can create content in separate Flash movies that load into the main movie, as viewers move through the site.

For our Gallery slideshow, we'll create a movie that builds its interface on the fly by parsing an XML file. Maintaining descriptions of content in a separate file makes it easy to add and remove examples without editing and republishing the Flash movie.

Let's take a quick look at the XML file we'll use.

Choose File > Open.

In the Open dialog, navigate to the development_files directory. Change the Files of Type menu to All Files (*.*) (Windows) or All Files (Mac).

Select the file dataGallery.xml and click Open.

Without getting into the details of XML formatting, you should be able to discern the following:

The file contains a series of entries in the top-level category of displays, < displays >.

Within the displays category there are four 2nd level groups, called nodes, [n], in XML, for display types, < type >. Each type has a name attribute.

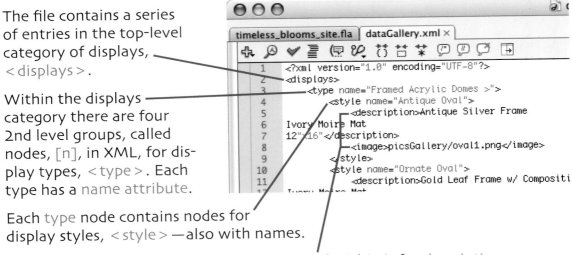

Each type node contains nodes for display styles, < style > —also with names.

Finally, each style node has two nodes nested within it for descriptions and images.

With that basic understanding, we're ready to work on the Flash movie that will use the XML.

load xml content (cont.)

Open the file contentGallery.fla. To speed our task, the file already has four named layers and a background layout upon which we'll build the gallery.

Select the layer xml connector.

From the Components panel Data list, drag out an instance of XML Connector and place it off the left edge of the Stage.

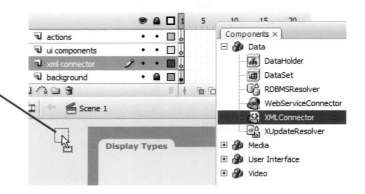

The XML Connector serves as a go-between, bringing data in from the XML file and broadcasting out to UI components that use the data to determine their displays.

Although it would not be visible in the movie if placed on the Stage, it's common to place it just off the top-left corner so it doesn't cause visual clutter or interfere with access to other objects in your document.

Set these values in the Parameters tab in the Property Inspector.

Instance Name: xcGallery

URL: dataGallery.xml

Direction: Receive

Select Frame 1 in the actions layer.

Open the Behaviors panel.

Click the Add Behavior button and choose Date > Trigger Data Source.

In the Trigger Data Source dialog select xcGallery and click OK.

add inside sections of the web site

Select the XML connector xcGallery.

We'll be working extensively in the Component Inspector panel so expand the panel dock to keep it open.

In the Component Inspector click the Schema tab.

In the scroll pane, select results : XML.

Click the Import a schema from a sample XML file button, in the upper-right corner of the Schema tab.

In the Open dialog, select dataGallery.xml and click Open.

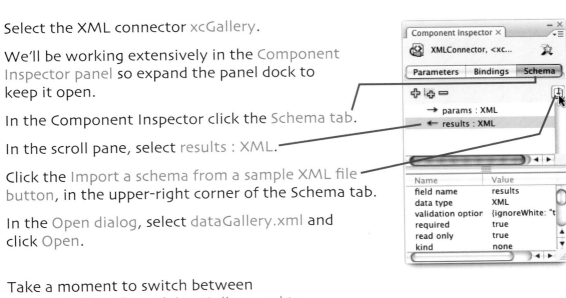

Take a moment to switch between contentGallery.fla and dataGallery.xml to see how the tag structures in the XML are parsed into the hierarchical data properties in the Schema tab.

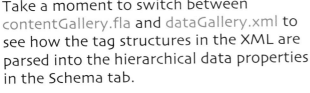

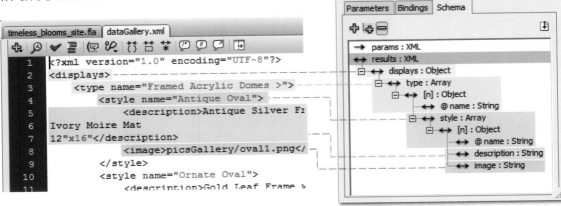

Close the file dataGallery.xml.

Save the file contentGallery.fla.

We have the process in place to import the XML. Now let's set up a user interface to use it.

add inside sections of the web site

use ui components

Select the layer ui components.

From the Components panel User Interface list, drag an instance of the List component onto the Stage. Place it on the green background, below the Display Types heading.

In the Property Inspector, set these values:

Instance Name: listDisplays

W: 145

H: 80

X: 25

Y: 40

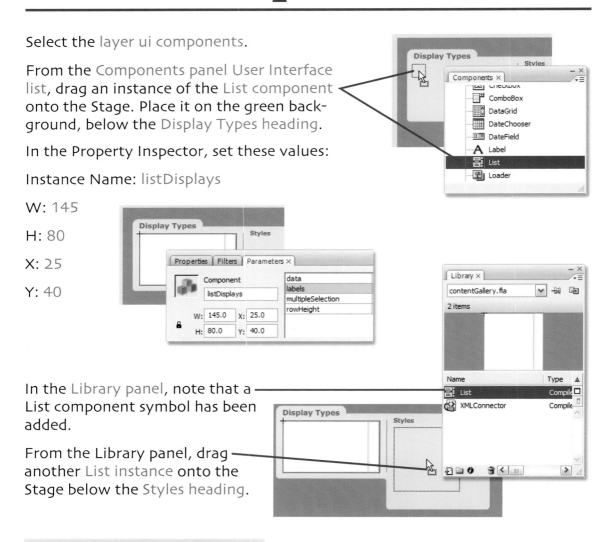

In the Library panel, note that a List component symbol has been added.

From the Library panel, drag another List instance onto the Stage below the Styles heading.

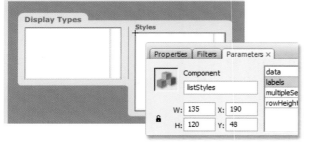

Give the List the Instance Name of listStyles, dimensions of W: 135 X H: 120, and location of X: 190 and Y: 48.

add inside sections of the web site

Next drag an instance of the Text Area component from the Components panel, placing it over the light purple background.

Set properties to an Instance Name of descStyles, W: 205 X H: 75, and X: 120 and Y: 250.

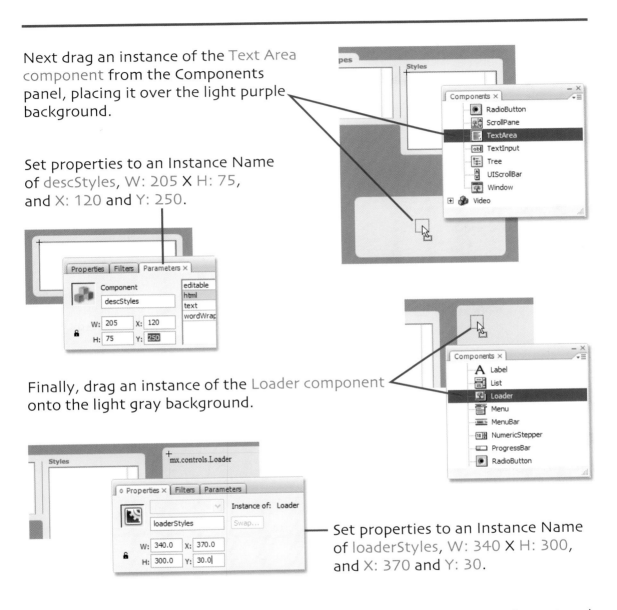

Finally, drag an instance of the Loader component onto the light gray background.

Set properties to an Instance Name of loaderStyles, W: 340 X H: 300, and X: 370 and Y: 30.

OK, now we have an XML file providing data, an XML Connector to import and distribute the data, and User Interface elements ready to be driven by the data. We just need to establish all of the connections.

bind data to the ui

When we connect a piece of data from an XML file to a user interface element, it's known as binding the data. Binding each piece of data to a component, via the XML Connector, is a multistep process. We bind the data to the XML Connector and specify to which UI component the connector will broadcast the data. Then we bind the incoming data to the component and specify how it will be handled.

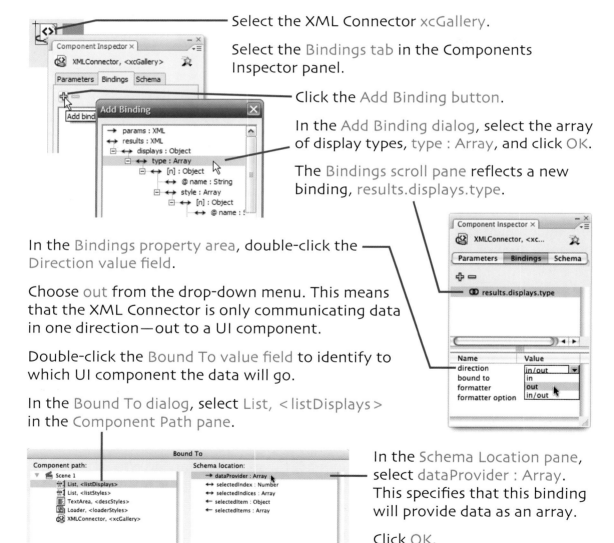

Select the XML Connector xcGallery.

Select the Bindings tab in the Components Inspector panel.

Click the Add Binding button.

In the Add Binding dialog, select the array of display types, type : Array, and click OK.

The Bindings scroll pane reflects a new binding, results.displays.type.

In the Bindings property area, double-click the Direction value field.

Choose out from the drop-down menu. This means that the XML Connector is only communicating data in one direction—out to a UI component.

Double-click the Bound To value field to identify to which UI component the data will go.

In the Bound To dialog, select List, < listDisplays > in the Component Path pane.

In the Schema Location pane, select dataProvider : Array. This specifies that this binding will provide data as an array.

Click OK.

Next, we'll repeat the bindings process for the style node and the two style objects—description and image.

With the XML Connector still selected, click the Add Binding button.

Select style : Array and click OK.

A new binding, results.displays.type.[n].style, is listed in the panel.

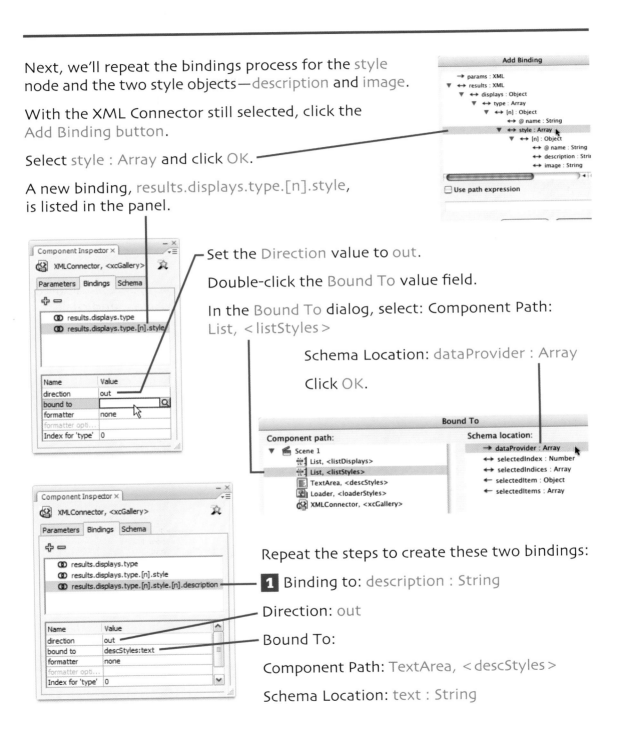

Set the Direction value to out.

Double-click the Bound To value field.

In the Bound To dialog, select: Component Path: List, <listStyles>

Schema Location: dataProvider : Array

Click OK.

Repeat the steps to create these two bindings:

1 Binding to: description : String

Direction: out

Bound To:

Component Path: TextArea, <descStyles>

Schema Location: text : String

bind data to the ui (cont.)

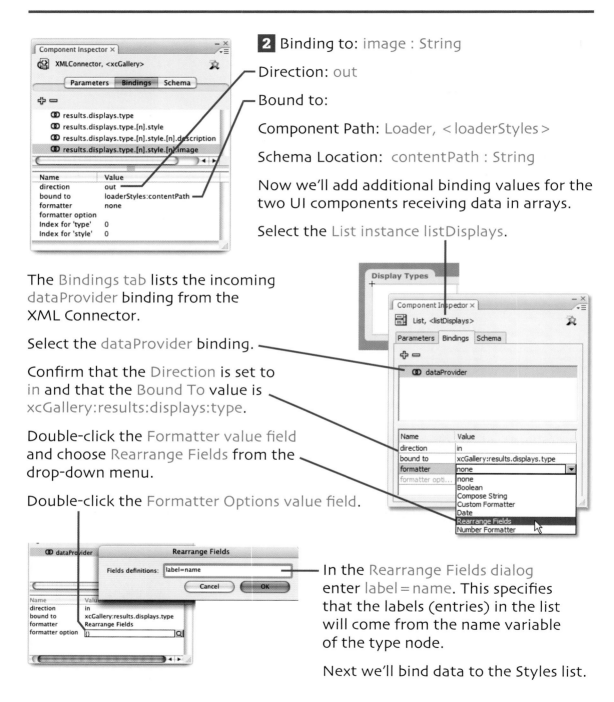

2 Binding to: image : String

Direction: out

Bound to:

Component Path: Loader, < loaderStyles >

Schema Location: contentPath : String

Now we'll add additional binding values for the two UI components receiving data in arrays.

Select the List instance listDisplays.

The Bindings tab lists the incoming dataProvider binding from the XML Connector.

Select the dataProvider binding.

Confirm that the Direction is set to in and that the Bound To value is xcGallery:results:displays:type.

Double-click the Formatter value field and choose Rearrange Fields from the drop-down menu.

Double-click the Formatter Options value field.

In the Rearrange Fields dialog enter label = name. This specifies that the labels (entries) in the list will come from the name variable of the type node.

Next we'll bind data to the Styles list.

Select the List instance listStyles.

In the Bindings panel, confirm Direction is in and Bound To is xcGallery:results: displays:type:[n]:style.

Double-click the Formatter value field and choose Rearrange Fields from the drop-down menu.

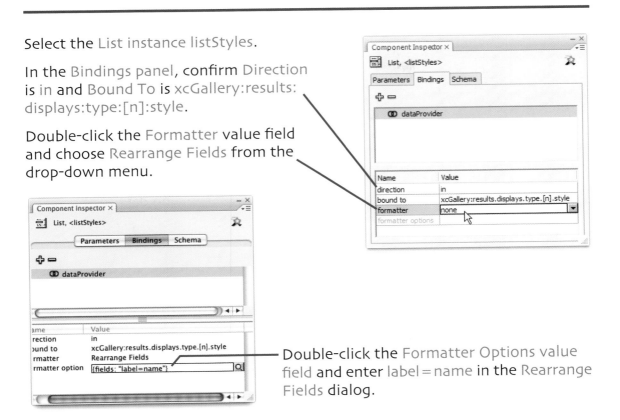

Double-click the Formatter Options value field and enter label = name in the Rearrange Fields dialog.

Let's take a look at what we've done so far.

Test the movie, [Ctrl][↵Enter] (Windows) or [⌘][↵Enter] (Mac).

All of our UI elements are now displaying content. It's a great start, but there's no connection between the elements and no response to making a selection in one of the lists.

We'll change that next.

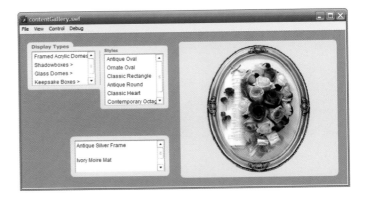

set ui interactions

For our UI to function correctly we need the Styles list to respond to selections in the Display Types list and for the description and image to respond to selections in the Styles list. We'll set up these interactions now.

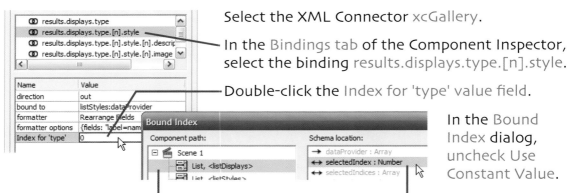

Select the XML Connector xcGallery.

In the Bindings tab of the Component Inspector, select the binding results.displays.type.[n].style.

Double-click the Index for 'type' value field.

In the Bound Index dialog, uncheck Use Constant Value.

Select List, < listDisplays > in the Component Path pane and selectedIndex : Number in the Schema Location pane.

Click OK.

In the Component Inspector, confirm that the Index for 'type' value shows listDisplays:selectedIndex.

This has bound listStyles to the selection in listDisplays.

Select the binding results.displays. type.[n].style.[n].description.

Double-click the Index for 'type' value field, uncheck Use Constant Value, and select Component Path : List, < listDisplays > and Schema Location : selectedIndex : Number in the dialog.

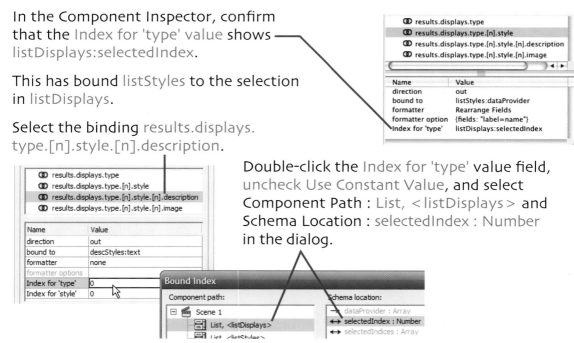

Confirm that the Index for 'type' value is set to listDisplays:selected Index.

Double-click the Index for 'style' value field, uncheck Use Constant Value, and select Component Path : List, < listStyles > and Schema Location : selectedIndex : Number in the dialog.

Click OK.

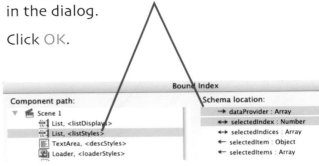

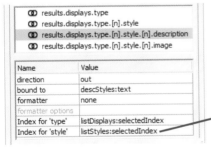

Confirm that the Index for 'style' value is set to listStyles:selected Index.

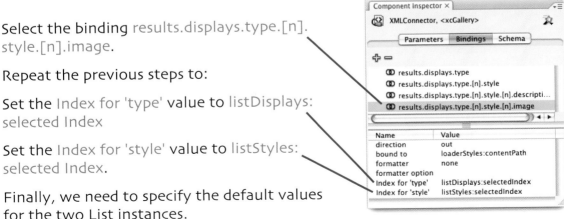

Select the binding results.displays.type.[n]. style.[n].image.

Repeat the previous steps to:

Set the Index for 'type' value to listDisplays: selected Index

Set the Index for 'style' value to listStyles: selected Index.

Finally, we need to specify the default values for the two List instances.

add inside sections of the web site

set ui interactions (cont.)

Select the List instance listDisplays.

Select the Schema tab in the Component Inspector panel.

Select the selectedIndex : Number property.

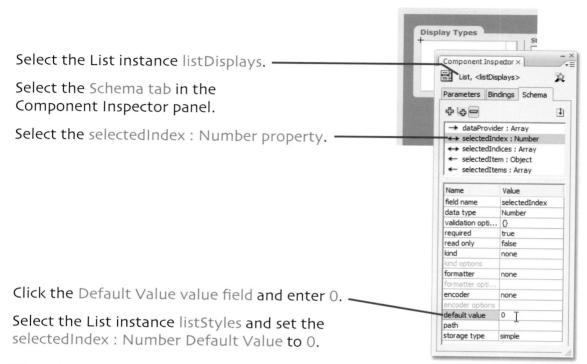

Click the Default Value value field and enter 0.

Select the List instance listStyles and set the selectedIndex : Number Default Value to 0.

That's it! Test the movie and explore your fully functioning Displays Gallery.

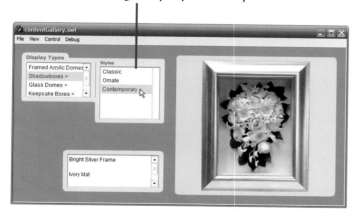

Close the Flash Player window.

When we test a movie, Flash exports a SWF movie file to play in the Flash Player, placing it in the same directory as the Flash file. Since we have no special publishing requirements for this movie, we can use that SWF to load into our main movie.

Save the Flash file contentGallery.fla.

load external movies

Back in our main Flash file (timeless_blooms_site.fla), we need to set up the file to load the contentGallery.swf movie into the Gallery section.

Select the keyframe gallery in the gallery content layer.

From the Components panel, drag an instance of the Loader component onto the Stage.

In the Parameters tab of the Property Inspector, name the symbol instance loaderGallery. Set the position x: 20 and y: 115.

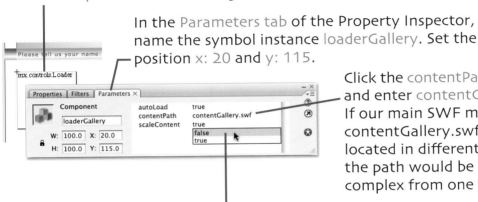

Click the contentPath value field and enter contentGallery.swf. If our main SWF movie and contentGallery.swf were to be located in different directories, the path would be more complex from one to the other.

Double-click the scaleContent parameter value field, and select false in the drop-down menu. This instructs Flash to display our movie at its actual size, not sizing it to the 100 X 100 dimensions of the Loader symbol.

Choose Control > Test Movie, or press [Ctrl][←Enter] (Windows) or [⌘][←Enter] (Mac). When the movie appears in the Flash Player window, click the Gallery button.

You see that our contentGallery movie with its XML-driven gallery is displayed in the content area exactly as we wanted.

Close the Flash Player window.

That's it. Our Gallery section is created and fully functional within our main site movie.

form components

Forms provide a common function in Web pages, providing a way for users to interact with the businesses and people behind a site. For our Pricing section we will create the basic framework of a form using components. To function properly and transfer data as intended, a form requires advanced ActionScript programming and connection to a database—complexity that is beyond the scope of this book. We'll limit our exercise to establishing the basics.

Select keyframe Pricing in the pricing content layer.

From the Library panel, drag out an instance of the symbol bkgd Sections > bkgdPricing. Again, to speed our task the symbol already has three named layers and a background layout upon which we'll place the form objects.

Position the symbol at x: 20 and y: 115.

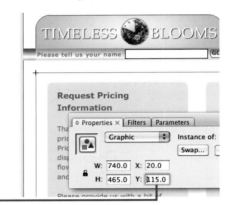

Double-click the bkgdPricing instance to invoke symbol-editing mode.

Select the ui components layer.

From the Components panel, drag out an instance of the TextInput component. Place the instance next to the label Name.

Name the instance inputName.

Set the width to 220 px.

Drag out another TextInput instance, placing it next to E-mail Address.

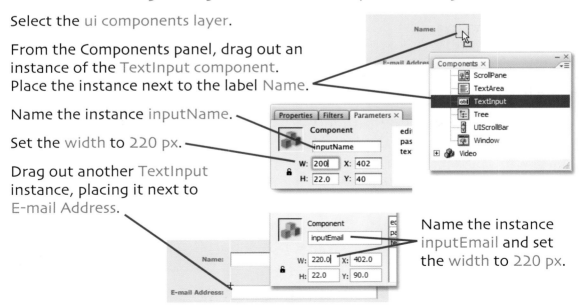

Name the instance inputEmail and set the width to 220 px.

add inside sections of the web site

Drag out an instance of the RadioButton component and place it next to Event.

In the Parameters tab, name the instance radioWedding.

Click to select the groupName parameter and enter groupEvent, identifying this radio button as part of a group containing other radio buttons we haven't yet placed.

Click to select the label parameter and enter Wedding.

Choose true from the selected parameter drop-down menu.

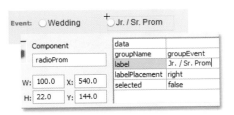

Drag out another RadioButton instance to the right of the Wedding RadioButton.

Set the Instance Name to radioProm, group-Name to groupEvent, and label to Jr. / Sr. Prom.

Place another RadioButton instance below Wedding and name it radioAnniversary. Set groupName to groupEvent and label to Anniversary Party.

Change the width to 110 to show the entire label.

Place a final RadioButton below Jr. / Sr. Prom and name it radioQuinceanera. Set groupName to groupEvent and label to Quinceanera.

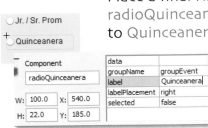

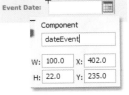

Drag an instance of the DateField component next to Event Date.

Name the instance dateEvent.

form components (cont.)

Drag an instance of the ComboBox component below the display type statement.

Name the instance comboDisplay and set the width to 155.

Double-click the labels parameter field.

In the dialog, click the Add New Value button four times.

Select the Value field for list item 0 and enter Framed Acrylic Domes. Set the other three values to Shadowboxes, Glass Domes, and Keepsake Boxes.

Click OK.

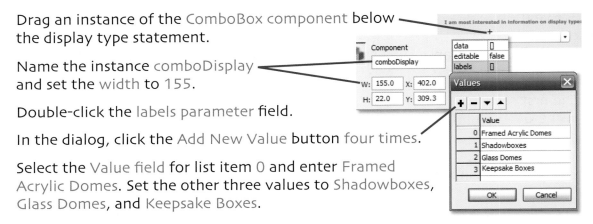

Drag an instance of the CheckBox component below the Combo Box and name the instance checkMailing.

Set the label to Please add me to your mailing list..

Set selected to true.

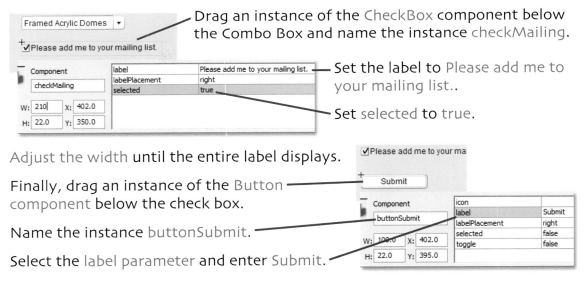

Adjust the width until the entire label displays.

Finally, drag an instance of the Button component below the check box.

Name the instance buttonSubmit.

Select the label parameter and enter Submit.

With all the components now placed, take a few moments to use the Align panel to perfect the layout.

Test the Movie and see how the different components operate.

Close the Flash Player.

That's it for our inside sections. Next, we'll work on modifying the appearance of the UI components to more closely match the appearance of our site.

add inside sections of the web site

skins and appearance

We've used several UI components in our site now, but their appearances don't necessarily match the visual style of our site. Using ActionScript, we can modify the overall appearance, known as the skin, and specify other style elements such as font family, size, and color.

The first set of customizations we'll implement are specific to the components in the Gallery file, so we'll put the ActionScript in that file.

Switch back to or open contentGallery.fla.

Select Frame 1 in the actions layer and enter code in the Actions panel as shown.

```
1
2      // Trigger Data Source Behavior
3      // Macromedia 2003
4      this.xcGallery.trigger();
5
6      // hide the vertical scroll bar area in the components
7      listDisplays.vScrollPolicy = "off";
8      listStyles.vScrollPolicy = "off";
9      descStyles.vScrollPolicy = "off";
10
11     // hide the borders
12     listDisplays.setStyle("borderStyle","none");
13     listStyles.setStyle("borderStyle","none");
14     descStyles.setStyle("borderStyle","none");
15
16     // change the background colors to match the
17     //backgrounds behind them
18     listDisplays.setStyle("backgroundColor",0xddeedd);
19     listStyles.setStyle("backgroundColor",0xddeedd);
20     descStyles.setStyle("backgroundColor", 0xeeddee);
21
22     // right align the text in the Display Types list
23     listDisplays.setStyle("textAlign", "right");
```

Test the movie and see how the Gallery components look now.

The text doesn't look as good as we'd like, but we'll change that in the main site movie.

Close the Flash Player.

Save and close contentGallery.fla.

add inside sections of the web site   **125**

skins and appearance (cont.)

Flash uses a construct called skins to describe the general appearance of UI components. Developers can create and use their own or can choose to use one of the variations of the default skin known as Halo. The green color you've seen around the UI in our movies, like the highlight color in the lists in the Gallery, are from the green variation of Halo. We'll change it to orange.

Back in the file timeless_blooms_site.fla, select keyframe intro in the actions layer.

In the Actions panel enter the code shown to change the Halo theme.

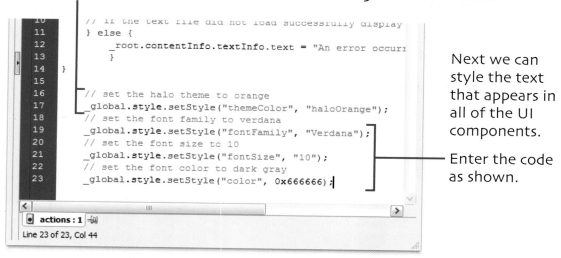

```
10    // if the text file did not load successfully display
11    } else {
12        _root.contentInfo.textInfo.text = "An error occurr
13    }
14    }
15
16    // set the halo theme to orange
17    _global.style.setStyle("themeColor", "haloOrange");
18    // set the font family to verdana
19    _global.style.setStyle("fontFamily", "Verdana");
20    // set the font size to 10
21    _global.style.setStyle("fontSize", "10");
22    // set the font color to dark gray
23    _global.style.setStyle("color", 0x666666);
```

actions : 1

Line 23 of 23, Col 44

Next we can style the text that appears in all of the UI components.

Enter the code as shown.

Test the movie and check out the UI components in the Gallery and Pricing sections, even the text input field for the visitor's name.

Our site sections are complete!

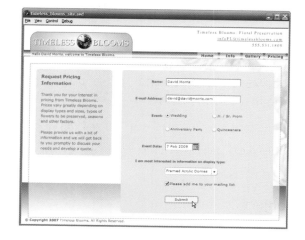

add inside sections of the web site

9. use flash video

Video is one of the most popular trends on the Web and Flash offers truly unmatched video capabilities. Many of the most well-known sites offering video use the Flash Player for delivery because of the compression available in the Flash Video (FLV) format, the flexibility of playback controls, and the ability to synch events in a Flash movie with points in the video files.

In this chapter you'll learn to:

Listen for cue point triggers to execute other actions in the Flash movie.

Use named cue points to dynamically alter text.

Use the Flash Video Import Wizard to convert videos to the Flash Video format.

Use ActionScript to dynamically change the visibility of objects.

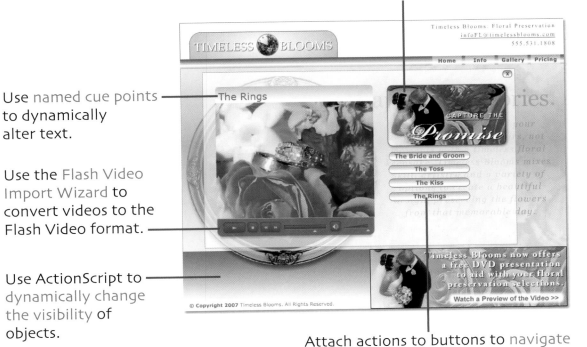

Attach actions to buttons to navigate to cue points in the video.

video playback area

Our video will display in a "video screen" area made visible with the click of a button. Before we import the video, we'll lay out the video screen and set up the button interaction.

In the main Timeline of timeless_blooms_site.fla, add a new layer above layer buttons. Name the new layer video.

Select Frame 11 in layer video and insert a keyframe (F6).

Select Frame 21 and insert a keyframe.

Click back in Keyframe 11.

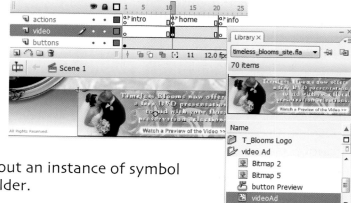

From the Library panel, drag out an instance of symbol videoAd from the video Ad folder.

Place the instance in the bottom-right corner of the Stage.

Drag an instance of symbol video-Screen from the video Screen folder. The basic elements of the video screen have been laid out in advance, allow-ing us to concentrate on video tasks.

In the Property Inspector, name the instance videoScreen.

Enter X: 0.0 and Y: 95.0.

The videoScreen symbol will not be visible when our Web site first loads. Viewers will click a button in videoAd to see it. Let's set up that action now.

use flash video

In the Timeline, select keyframe home in the actions layer.

In the Actions panel, make sure that Script Assist is not selected.

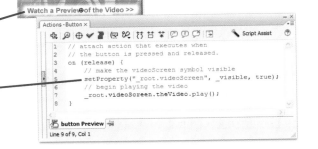

Enter the code as shown below the stop action to make the video screen invisible when the frame loads.

Double-click the symbol instance videoAd to invoke symbol-editing mode.

Click the text Watch a Preview of the Video >> to select the symbol button Preview.

In the Actions panel, enter the code as shown here.

Note that commented code, preceded by //, is instructive text to show you what the code does.

In the Library panel, double-click the videoScreen symbol icon to invoke symbol-editing mode.

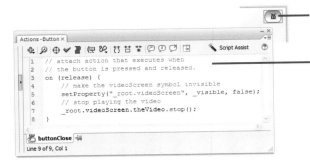

Select the X button in the top-right corner.

Enter the code as shown to close the video screen and stop video playback.

Note that if our video had audio and we didn't stop the playback, the video would continue to play and viewers would still hear the audio.

use flash video

import video

With our video screen layout in place, we can import our video file—converting it to the Flash Video (FLV) format and inserting cue points. Cue points, placed at specified times, provide markers to which the Playback Head can be sent via ActionScript and trigger events elsewhere in the Flash movie as the Playback Head passes over them. (See extra bits on Page 136.)

Still in symbol-editing mode on the videoScreen symbol, select layer video in the Timeline.

Select File > Import > Import Video to launch the Flash Video Import Wizard.

In the Select Video pane, click the Browse button under the On your computer selection.

Navigate to the development_files folder. Select videoWedding.mov and click Open.

Back in the Select Video pane, click Next.

In the Deployment pane, select Progressive download from a web server and click Next.

Select the Video tab in the Encoding pane and select High from the Quality drop-down menu.

The video doesn't have any sound, so we'll skip the Audio setting.

Select the Cue Points tab.

Here we'll embed cue points at different points in the video. Later we'll be able to synch actions in our Flash movie with the cue points and to configure buttons for navigating to them.

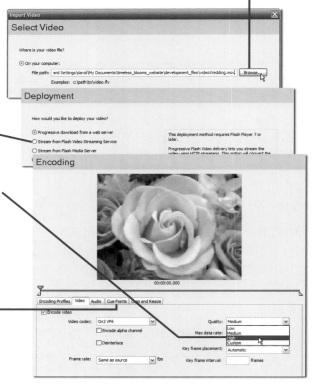

use flash video

Click the Add Cue Point button.

In the Name field, enter
The Bride and Groom.

In the Type drop-down menu,
select Navigation.

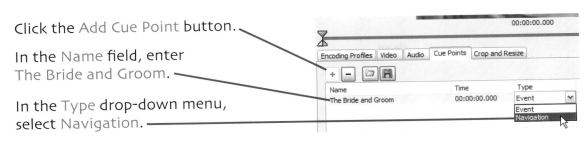

Enter cue point names carefully, they must match exactly some Frame Labels
in a Movie Clip symbol that we'll work with shortly.

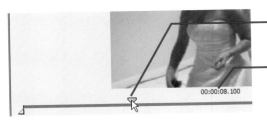

Click and drag the Playback Head to the
right, progressing through the video.

Just past the 8-second mark, there is an
edit switching from the bride and groom
to a clip of the bouquet toss.

Release the Playback Head as close to the edit as you can.

Use the left and right arrow keys on your keyboard to more precisely place the
Playback Head at the edit.

Click the Add Cue Point button and
enter The Toss as the Name. Set the
Type to Navigation.

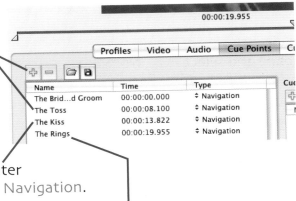

Drag the Playback Head further to
the right until you see the bouquet
toss clip dissolve to a clip of the
couple kissing.

Click the Add Cue Point button and enter
The Kiss as the Name. Set the Type to Navigation.

Finally, move the Playback Head to the point where
that clip dissolves to an image of wedding rings.

Add a cue point named The Rings, with Type set to Navigation.

Click Next.

use flash video

import video (cont.)

In the Skinning pane, we choose the control types and appearance attached to the video.

From the Skin drop-down menu, choose SteelExternalAll.swf. This means we want the steel appearance, outside the video image, and we want all available controls.

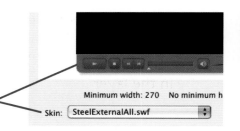

Minimum width: 270   No minimum h

Skin: SteelExternalAll.swf

Read the messages in the Finish Video Import pane and click Finish.

Wait as Flash converts the original QuickTime video file to an FLV file, embeds the cue points, adds the playback controls, and attaches the movie to an FLVPlayback component.

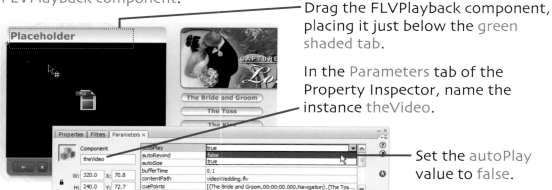

Drag the FLVPlayback component, placing it just below the green shaded tab.

In the Parameters tab of the Property Inspector, name the instance theVideo.

Set the autoPlay value to false.

Examine the different elements in the videoScreen symbol.

The Dynamic text box headerCue will display cue point names as the video plays. The movie clip videoBanner has four keyframes with frame labels that match exactly the cue point Names. Cue points will trigger moves between the keyframes.

The four buttons will move the video playhead to the matching cue points.

Click Scene 1 in the Edit Bar to exit symbol-editing mode.

Test your movie. From the Home section, click the button in the ad to open the video screen and watch the video play.

Close the Flash Player.

cue point triggers

To respond to the cue points in the video, we'll set up ActionScript "listeners" that will listen for the cue points and then execute actions we specify.

Select keyfame Home in the layer actions.

In the Actions panel, enter the code as shown here.

Review the commented code to understand what each piece of code does.

```
1    stop();
2
3    setProperty("_root.videoScreen", _visible, false);
4
5    // create a variable for an event listener
6    var cueListener:Object = new Object();
7    // declare a function called by the event listener
8    // the listener passes a reference to the cue point
9    cueListener.cuePoint = function(cues) {
10       // create a variable for the name of the cue point
11       var cueName = cues.info.name;
12       // replace the text Placeholder in the dynamic
13       // text container with the name of the cue point
14       _root.videoScreen.textClip.text = cueName;
15       // move the video banner movieclip to the named
16       // keyframe that matches the cue name
17       _root.videoScreen.videoBanner.gotoAndStop(cueName);
18    }
19    // start the event listener
20    _root.videoScreen.theVideo.addEventListener("cuePoint", cueListener);
```

Actions - Frame ×

Script Assist

actions : 11

Line 14 of 21, Col 28

Test your movie. From the Home section, click the button in the ad to open the video screen and watch the video play.

Note that the header text Placeholder is replaced by the cue point names as the video plays past each cue point.

Also, note that the phrase in the banner graphic changes each time a cue point is passed.

Excellent! Now let's set up the button navigation.

Close the Flash Player.

cue point navigation

Finally, for the presentation of our video let's attach actions to the buttons in the video screen that will allow viewers to navigate to the different points in the video.

Double-click the videoScreen symbol to invoke symbol-editing mode.

Select the button with the text The Bride and Groom.

In the Actions panel, click the Script Assist button to turn on assistance.

In the Actions Toolbox, locate and click Components to open the Components list.

Navigate to FLVPlayback > Methods and double-click seekToNavCuePoint.

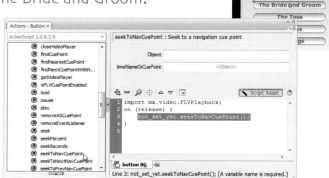

Code for an on release function and seekToNavCuePoint method is added in the Script pane.

With the method selected, click in the Object field in the Script Assist toolbar.

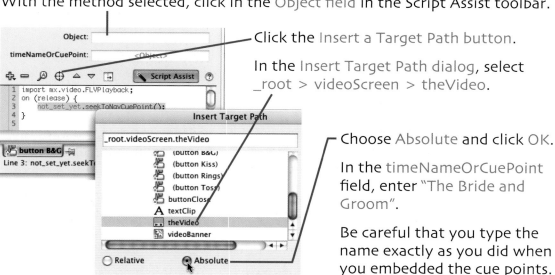

Click the Insert a Target Path button.

In the Insert Target Path dialog, select _root > videoScreen > theVideo.

Choose Absolute and click OK.

In the timeNameOrCuePoint field, enter "The Bride and Groom".

Be careful that you type the name exactly as you did when you embedded the cue points.

Initial releases of Flash CS3 Professional placed the code import mx.video. FLVPlayback in the wrong place and the action did not work. If your Actions panel has the import code on line 1, before on (release) {, follow Steps 1 and 2 to move the code. If not, proceed to Step 3.

1 In the Script pane, click in the first line of code. The entire line of code is selected. Right-click (Windows) or [Control]-click (Mac) and choose Cut from the drop-down menu.

2 Click in the line of code on (release) {, selecting the entire line. Paste the code from the clipboard.

3 We'll do a quick copy-and-paste process to add the code to the other three buttons.

In the Actions panel, click Script Assist to turn it off.

Select all of the code and copy it to the clipboard.

On the Stage, click to select the button labeled The Toss.

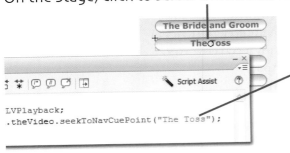

In the Actions pane, paste the code.

Change "The Bride and Groom" to "The Toss".

Repeat the process for the other two buttons, entering "The Kiss" and "The Rings".

Test your movie. From the Home section, click the button in the ad to open the video screen and watch the video play. Randomly click the buttons to move the Playback Head among the different cue points.

That's it! You've successfully imported Flash video, embedded cue points, and used those cue points to trigger ActionScript events and as navigation targets.

Close the Flash Player.

Our site development is complete and we're ready to publish to the Web.

use flash video

extra bits

import video p. 130

- For converting a single video file to the Flash File (FLV) format, we use the Flash Video Import wizard with the Flash authoring tool. The stand-alone application Flash Video Encoder, which is installed with Flash CS3 Professional, is better suited for converting multiple files in one sitting.

- If QuickTime 7 for Macintosh, QuickTime 6.5 for Windows, or DirectX 9 or later (Windows only) is installed on your system, you can import video clips in several file formats, including MOV, AVI, and MPG/MPEG. You can import linked video clips in MOV format.

- There are two types of cue points: event and navigation.

  Event cue points trigger actions when the cue point is reached, and synch the video playback to other events in the Flash movie.

  Navigation cue points are used for navigation and seeking, but can function secondarily like an Event cue.

  We use navigation cues in this exercise because we need the functionality of both types.

10. publish your web site

With development of all of our site sections complete, the only thing left to do is to ready our files for upload to the Web.

In this chapter we accomplish the following:

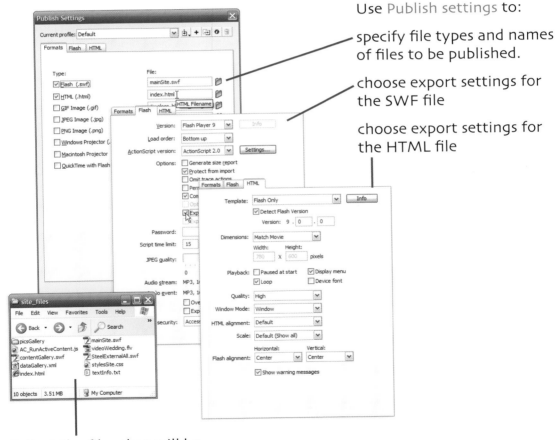

Use Publish settings to:

specify file types and names of files to be published.

choose export settings for the SWF file

choose export settings for the HTML file

Collect the files that will be uploaded to our Web server.

swf settings

In Flash, we have the opportunity to specify different attributes for the files we're going to publish. In this section, we'll determine the Publish Settings for our main site movie.

Choose File > Publish Settings, or click the Settings button in the Property Inspector. The Publish Settings dialog appears.

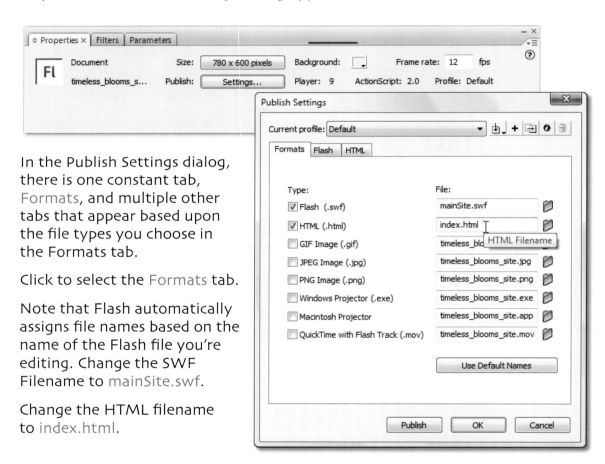

In the Publish Settings dialog, there is one constant tab, Formats, and multiple other tabs that appear based upon the file types you choose in the Formats tab.

Click to select the Formats tab.

Note that Flash automatically assigns file names based on the name of the Flash file you're editing. Change the SWF Filename to mainSite.swf.

Change the HTML filename to index.html.

Click the Flash tab. The Version drop-down menu defaults to the Flash Player version associated with the version of Flash you're using. In our case, that's Flash Player 9.

Load Order determines in what order the Flash Player draws layers as the movie loads. Set the Load Order to Bottom up.

Leave the ActionScript version set to ActionScript 2.0.

Protect from Import prevents other people from importing your SWF file into Flash — protecting your work from theft. Click to select this option.

Ignore the Omit Trace Actions and Permit Debugging options, as they are used for more advanced development than we've covered here.

Leave the Compress Movie option selected; it helps to reduce file size.

Select Export Hidden Layers.

Leave the Password field blank.

Leave the JPEG Quality setting at 80.

Our one sound file was optimized before import, so we don't need to change anything in the Audio settings.

Local Playback Security should be set to Access local files only.

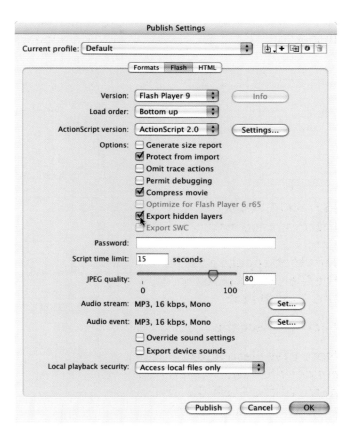

html settings

Flash movies on the Web need to be wrapped in HTML files that provide movie display instructions to the browser. The HTML files can also include code that checks for the presence of the correct Flash Player plug-in and redirects the viewer if it's not there.

Luckily for us, Flash can publish the HTML code we need so we don't have to do the coding ourselves.

Select the HTML tab.

Flash generates the HTML file from a set of customizable templates designed for different Flash delivery requirements.

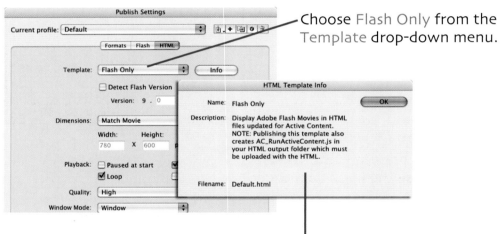

Choose Flash Only from the Template drop-down menu.

Click Info and read the description of this template. Note the content regarding Active Content and the addition of a JavaScript (.js) file to your export directory.

This is a VERY good thing. You may not know what Active Content is, but if you use Internet Explorer you've seen it. Have you noticed recently that when you enter a Web page with Flash content, the first time you click an element like a play button you have to click a second time to get it to register your click? That's Active Content, and the code Flash will export for us eliminates the user having to click twice.

Click OK to close the HTML Template Info dialog.

publish your web site

We want our file to test for the Flash plug-in and to provide an opportunity to install it if it isn't present. Click the check box to select Detect Flash Version.

The remaining options in the HTML tab allow users to customize how their movies appear and behave in the browser window. For our purposes the default settings are appropriate, so we won't make any changes.

Click the Publish button to generate the SWF movie file and the HTML file we've requested.

Click OK to close the dialog.

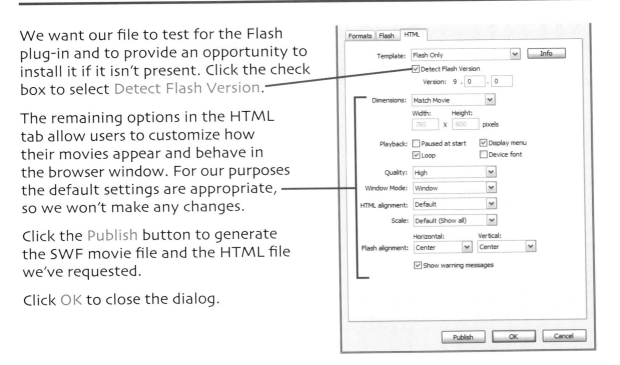

Save and close any files open in Flash. Choose File > Exit (Windows) or Flash > Quit Flash (Mac) to close the Flash application.

From your computer's Desktop, navigate to the development_files folder. You'll see that Flash has added the Flash movie (mainSite.swf) and the HTML file (index.html).

Double-click the file index.html to open it in the browser.

Because you have the correct plug-in (that was installed with the Flash application) you will see our completed site movie displayed. If you didn't have the plug-in, you would see alternative content with instructions to download it.

collect files for upload

Our final step is to collect all of the files that will be uploaded to your Web server and copy them into the site_files folder.

The following is a list of the files to copy, along with brief descriptions:

AC_RunActiveContent.js—JavaScript file that eliminates the need to click the first element twice

contentGallery.swf—Gallery section movie that includes XML parsing and bindings

dataGallery.xml—XML file that includes all of the tags describing items in the gallery

index.html— Page containing mainSite.swf; our site is displayed in this page; executes Flash Player detection and redirects, if necessary

mainSite.swf—our main site movie including the Home section, animated intro, inside sections, and video

newVideo.flv—Flash Video file, including cue points

SteelExternalAll.swf—Contains elements used in the video playback controls

stylesSite.css—Cascading Style Sheet used to format text in the Info section

textInfo.txt—file with HTML-formatted text for the Info section

picsGallery—Directory containing image files for the Gallery section

Once you've copied all of these files into the site_files folder, you're ready to upload them using your FTP application and instructions from your Web hosting company or Internet service provider.

When you're done uploading, be sure to view your site via a browser and confirm that everything is working as it should.

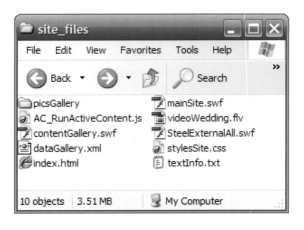

That's it! You've successfully created and published a Web site using Flash. Now you have the know-how to create attractive, useful Flash-based Web sites all on your own. Enjoy!

index

index

index

index

index

Pricing section, 122
primitive objects, 13–14
Property Inspector
    adjusting object shapes in, 13
    changing text spacing in, 23
    Corner Radius controls, 14
    Filters tab, 43
    hiding secondary controls
        in, xx
    opening, 4
    purpose of, xv
    setting Alpha in, 37
    setting text attributes in, 20
    viewing object hierarchies
        in, 32
Protect from Import option, 139
Publish Settings dialog, 137,
    138–139
publishing Web sites, 137–142
    collecting files, 142
    HTML settings, 140–141
    SWF settings, 138–139

Q

QuickTime versions, 136
QuickTime video files, 132

R

Radial Gradient fill, 18
RadioButton component, 123
Radius Handles, 14
Rearrange Fields command, 116
Rectangle Primitive tool, 13
Rectangle Primitives, 13–14
Rectangle tool, 11, 12
Registration Point markers, 69,
    70
Resize handle, 22, 23
reusable objects, 25, 26–27, 38.
    See also symbols
rotation handle, 16
round Resize handle, 20
rulers, 10

S

Save As dialog, 5
Save command, 5
saving
    color schemes, 7
    files, 5
    workspaces, 6
scenes, xiii, 32, 49
Schema tab, 111, 120
Script Assist button, 66, 101, 134
Script Assist mode, 50
scrolling text, 104–105
seekToNavCuePoint method,
    134
Select All command, 26
Selection tool, 15, 18, 31
shape tweens, 73
Show Guides command, 16, 35,
    40
Show/Hide Timeline button, 33
site_files folder, 2, 142
skins, 125–126, 132
Skip button, 73
Snap to Guides option, 10
sound, button, 87
span, keyframes, 49
square handle, 16, 17
square Resize handle, 22
Squeeze option, 59, 62
Stage
    changing view of, xv
    defining areas of, 10
    and film metaphor, xiii
    gray space around, xiv
    placing symbol instances on,
        26–27
    purpose of, xiv
    transforming objects on, 31
static text, 99
Static Text button, 20
SteelExternalAll.swf, 142
Stop action, 47, 48, 70, 84, 85
Stop command, 71
Stroke color well, 11, 12, 13, 24
style sheets, 108, 142
stylesSite.css, 142
Submit button, 124

Swap Symbol dialog, 90–91
SWF files, 3, 67
SWF settings, 138–139
symbol-editing mode, 30, 31,
    35, 38
Symbol Properties dialog, 98
symbol swapping, 88–91
symbols
    accessing, xvii
    benefits of using, 38, 96
    editing, 30
    importing, 96
    moving between layers, 34
    organizing, 29
    purpose of, xvii, 25
    storing, xvii
    updating, 97–98

T

T_Blooms Home Content.ai, 40,
    41
T_Blooms Logo folder, 29
templates, button, 78
Test Movie command, 67
text, 19–24. See also text boxes
    adding single line of, 20–21
    blurring, 55
    changing line spacing for, 23
    editing, 21
    loading HTML, 106–107
    scrolling, 104–105
    selecting, 21
    setting attributes for, 20
    setting dynamically, 101–103
    styling with CSS, 108
    underlining, 24
    zooming in/out, 56–62
Text Area component, 113
text boxes, 20–23
    closing, 22
    creating, 20
    editing text in, 21, 23
    fixed-width, 22
    repositioning, 23
    scrolling text in, 104–105
    types of, 99

index

Text (Fill) color control, 20
Text tool
    adding single line of text with, 20–21
    and button text, 80
    and dynamic text, 102
    and fixed-width text, 22
    and input text, 100
    and scrolling text, 104
    and Timeline Effects, 56
Text Type menu, 20
text wrap, 22, 23
textInfo.txt, 107, 108, 142
TextInput component, 122
Timeless Blooms Web site
    adding animation to, 51–74
    adding content to, 95–126
    adding copyright notice to, 21
    adding e-mail link to, 24
    adding sections to, 76–77
    adding text to, 19–21
    adding video playback area to, 128–129
    building navigation system for, 75–94
    defining folder structure for, 2
    downloading asset files for, 1
    home page for, viii, 40–41
    publishing, 137–142
timeless_blooms_site.fla, 5
timeless_blooms_website folder, 2
Timeline
    adding frames to, 39
    controlling, 47–48, 50
    defining frames in, 44, 49
    displaying frame labels in, 46
    purpose of, xiii, xvi
    setting active layer in, 34
    showing/hiding, 33
Timeline Effects, 56–62
Title Bar, 27
Tools panel, xv, 11
transformation handles, 17, 31
transforming objects, 31, 38

Transition effects, 68–69
transparency, 25, 37, 38. See also alpha transparency
Trigger Data Source behavior, 110
tween filter effects, 55
tweening, 73
tweens, 52–53, 73
TXT files, 106, 107, 108, 142
Type menu, 18

U

UI components, 112–126
    binding data to, 114–117
    downloading custom, xx
    modifying appearance of, 125–126
    setting interactions for, 118–120
    using, 112–113
UIScrollbar component, 105
Ulrich, Katherine, xix
Underline text style, 24
Up state, 79, 94
Update Library Items dialog, 98
URL Link field type, 24
user input, 99–100
user interface, xiii–xviii, xx. See also UI components
User Interface list, 112

V

variables, 100, 103
vector objects, 25, 28, 38
video, 127–136
    importance of, 127
    importing, 130–132, 136
    laying out video screen for, 128–129
    setting cue point triggers for, 133
    setting up navigation for, 134–135

W

Web site
    adding animation to, 51–74
    adding content to, 95–126
    adding copyright notice to, 21
    adding e-mail link to, 24
    adding sections to, 76–77
    adding text to, 19–21
    building navigation system for, 75–94
    choosing color scheme for, 8
    defining folder structure for, 2
    designing visual framework for, 9
    drawing background for, 11–12
    preparing files for, 1
    publishing, 137–142
    saving color scheme for, 7
    saving files for, 5
    this book's companion, xii, 1, 2, 28
    using video on, 127–136
Work Area command, xiv
workspaces, 6, 33
wrap, text, 22, 23

X

XML Connector, 110, 114–115, 118
XML files, 95, 109–111, 114, 142